BiBLe CRaFtS & MORE FOR AGES 2-4

STANDARD PUBLISHING
Cincinnati, Ohio

Bible Crafts & More for Ages 2-4

Standard Publishing, Cincinnati, Ohio
A division of Standex International Corporation
© 1999 by Standard Publishing
Printed in the United States of America

Credits

Cover design: Diana Walters
Inside illustrations: Lynne Davis
Project editor: Christine Spence
Acquisitions editor: Ruth Frederick

06 05 04 03 02   5 4

ISBN   0-7847-0974-2

Contents

contents

Contents

contents

Introduction

The following pages contain over 100 Bible crafts, plus an extra section of holiday and seasonal crafts! These crafts were designed especially for children ages two through four. Each craft is divided into sections to make it easy for you to use.

WHAT YOU NEED lists all the materials you will need to gather for the craft.

WHAT YOU DO lists numbered, step-by-step simple instructions for preparing and completing the craft.

WHAT YOU TALK ABOUT lists two or three simple conversation starters that relate the craft to the Bible story.

WANT TO DO MORE? is an optional section that contains rhymes, songs, or extra suggestions for the craft.

The crafts are arranged in biblical order. Look in the Table of Contents to find a particular Scripture or story. If you are searching for a particular type of craft, look in the index on pages 155, 156. If you are using Standard Publishing's 2's and 3's Sunday school curriculum, look on pages 157-160 to find the crafts that correlate with each Bible story.

Craft Recipes

BUBBLES

⅓ c. dish soap or baby shampoo
1¼ c. water
2 tsp. sugar
1 drop food coloring

Combine ingredients and pour into an unbreakable bottle.

SILLY PUTTY

1 cup Elmer's Glue-All
⅓ cup Sta-Flo laundry starch
Food coloring (optional)
Scent oil or extract (optional)
Pour starch into a bowl. Add food coloring and scent if desired. Slowly pour the glue into the starch. Stir the mixture as glue is added. The mixture should begin to clump together.

Let mixture rest three to five minutes. Then pour onto a cookie sheet or counter top and knead for several minutes. If mixture is sticky, add a small amount of starch. The putty should not stick to fingers or the playing surface. Store in an airtight container in the refrigerator.

FLUBBER

Mix 1½ cups warm water with 2 cups white glue in a bowl.

In a second bowl, mix 1⅓ cups warm water with 3 tsp. Borax. Add food coloring if desired.

Pour Borax mixture into glue mixture. Use a metal spoon to lift and turn mixture until only 1 tsp. of liquid remains. Pour off excess liquid. Store in an airtight container.

GOOP

½ c. cornstarch
¼ c. water
Food coloring or tempera
Trays, bowls, spoons

Mix cornstarch, water, and food coloring. Pour onto trays or into a plastic tub. Allow children to explore!

PLAY DOUGH

1 cup flour
1 cup water
1 cup salt
1 Tbsp. cream of tartar
Food coloring, tempera powder, Jell-O, or Kool-Aid

Mix all ingredients and cook on low until mixture forms a ball. Knead until smooth. Store in an airtight container.

CLEAN MUD

2 rolls toilet paper
1 cup Borax
1 bar soap
1 potato peeler
Red, green, and yellow food coloring
Water

Over a large bowl, begin to unroll toilet paper and tear into pieces. Scrape bar of soap with peeler until gone. Pour in 1 cup of Borax. Add 4 cups of water. Continue to mix and tear. Add red, green, and yellow food coloring to make mixture brown. Add more water as needed.

Creation Wall Hanging

WHAT YOU NEED

Paper plates
Yarn
Glue
Colorful wrapping paper
Crayons
Marker
Hole punch

WHAT YOU DO

1. Punch a hole in each paper plate. Insert a 3" piece of yarn and tie a knot to make a hanger. Print "God made the earth and sky" on the plates.

2. Cut 3" circles from wrapping paper. Fringe the edges of the circles by making ¼" cuts around the edges. See the illustration.

3. Guide children to glue the flowers on the plates. Give children green crayons and show them how to draw stems on their flowers.

WHAT YOU TALK ABOUT

Point to your flowers. What color are they?
Who made the flowers?

Leaf Prints

WHAT YOU NEED
Sponges
Spring-type clothespins
Tempera paint
Aluminum pie pans
Manila paper
Newspaper
Paint smocks
Leaf pattern from page 140

WHAT YOU DO

1. Cut leaves out of sponges, using the pattern on page 140. Attach a clothespin to each sponge for a handle.

2. Mix various autumn colors of tempera paint. You may wish to add liquid detergent to the paint to make it washable. Put the paint in aluminum pie pans. Put a sponge in each pan of paint.

3. Cover tables with newspaper. Help children put on paint smocks. Show the children how to press their leaf sponges on the large sponge to get just enough paint.

WHAT YOU TALK ABOUT
How many leaves are on your paper?
Who made the leaves?

Touch-and-Feel Bird

WHAT YOU NEED
Construction paper
Craft sticks
Glue
Felt or other fuzzy material
Crayons
Marker
Bird and wing patterns from
page 140

WHAT YOU DO

1 Cut birds out of construction paper and wings out of a contrasting color of felt.

2 Help children glue two craft sticks together, overlapping the ends. Then help them glue wings on their birds and glue the birds to the craft-stick perches.

3 Print "God made the animals" on the craft sticks. Let children use crayons to color eyes on their birds.

WHAT YOU TALK ABOUT
Who made the birds?
What other animals did God make?

God Made the Animal

Glitter colors

WHAT YOU NEED

Red, green, blue, and yellow
tempera paint
Four small sponges
Glitter
Disposable pie pans
Raw, unpeeled potatoes
White construction paper
Black marker
Painting smocks
Star, flower, and bird patterns from
page 126

WHAT YOU DO

1 Add glitter to the different colors of paint or pur-
chase glitter paint. Pour a small amount of each color
of paint in a disposable pie pan. Place a small sponge
in each pan of paint.

2 Cut potatoes in half and draw a simple design on the
cut half. Use the star, bird, and flower patterns from
page 126, as well as other simple shapes. Cut away
the part of the potato around the design to make a
paint stamp. Put at least one potato pattern with
each color of paint.

3 Give children the painting smocks and white paper.
Show the children how to press the potato to the
paint sponge and then press it onto their paper to
make a print. Encourage children to use several different colors and stamps to make a colorful design.

WHAT YOU TALK ABOUT

What colors that God made do you see?
Point to a color God made.
Say, "Thank You, God."

Fuzzy Sheep

WHAT YOU NEED

White poster board (or corrugated
   cardboard)
Cotton balls
Glue
Black crayons or markers
Sheep pattern from page 126

WHAT YOU DO

1. Cut two sheep for each child from white poster board. Also cut two 1" x 2" strips of poster board for each child.

2. Glue the strips of poster board between the two sheep, so they will stand up.

3. Help the children draw on the sheep's eyes and glue cotton to the outer sides of the sheep.

WHAT YOU TALK ABOUT

How does your sheep feel?
Who made soft sheep for us to feel?

Snack Trays

WHAT YOU NEED

Styrofoam egg carton, one per child
Fun stickers or crayons
Permanent marker
Foods to taste (fresh fruit cut in
  bite-size pieces, small crackers,
  miniature marshmallows, cubes
  of cheese, sunflower seeds)
Containers in which to store the
  food
Spoons

WHAT YOU DO

1. Put each food into a separate container. Thoroughly wash egg cartons.

2. Help children decorate the tops of their cartons with stickers or crayons.

3. Ask children to wash their hands before eating. Then allow them to select a little of each food and place this in the egg spaces.

WHAT YOU TALK ABOUT

What is your favorite food to taste?
Who made foods for us to taste?

WANT TO DO MORE?

Provide child-size mini-muffin tins and allow children to decorate them to make a more durable snack tray. Allow children to take their snack trays home and use them to taste wonderful foods God made.

Potpourri Sachets

WHAT YOU NEED

Envelopes
Potpourri
Stickers and crayons
Scented potpourri oil (provide two
    or three different scents)

WHAT YOU DO

1. Give children the envelopes and ask them to use stickers and crayons to decorate their envelopes.

2. Help the children put a few spoonfuls of potpourri in their envelopes. Then put a few drops of oil in each child's potpourri. Allow them to choose which scent you use.

3. Help children seal their envelopes.

WHAT YOU TALK ABOUT

Who made things for us to smell?
Let's say, "Thank You, God."
You can put your envelope in your drawer at home.

Cymbals

WHAT YOU NEED

Plastic lids from eight-ounce
    margarine containers
Empty thread spools
Glue
Construction paper
Stickers of children and/or music
    notes

WHAT YOU DO

1. Cut out construction-paper circles to fit the insides of the plastic lids. Prepare two lids, two circles of paper, and have two spools for each child.

2. Help children glue the paper circles into the lids, center the spools, and glue them onto the covered lids. Then allow them to decorate the cymbals with stickers.

WHAT YOU TALK ABOUT

What is your favorite song about Jesus?
Let's tap our cymbals together as we sing.
Who made wonderful things for us to hear?

Paper Dolls

WHAT YOU NEED

Cardboard or tagboard
Fabric scraps
Crayons
Re-sticking tape (such as Post-it
 Note Tape from Scotch)
Dolls and clothing patterns from
 page 141

WHAT YOU DO

1. Cut paper dolls from white cardboard or tagboard. Cut out clothes for the dolls from fabric scraps, using the patterns on page 141.

2. Let children decorate their dolls with crayons and draw on faces if they wish. Help children glue pieces of re-sticking tape to the center of their dolls. These should be glued on with the sticky side up.

3. Let children choose clothing to stick on their dolls. The re-sticking tape will allow the children to put on and remove the clothing over and over.

WHAT YOU TALK ABOUT

Who made people?
What were the names of the first people God
 made?
Who made you?

Family Faces

WHAT YOU NEED

Construction paper
Scissors
Pictures of men, women, boys, and
   girls cut from magazines
Glue
Marker
House pattern from page 125

WHAT YOU DO

1 Cut one house for each child from the pattern on page 125.

2 Give the children the houses and allow them to choose pictures of people to glue in the house to make their families. Print "(name of child)'s family" on each child's house.

WHAT YOU TALK ABOUT

Who is in your family? Who lives at your house? Who gave us our families?

God's Care wreaths

WHAT YOU NEED
Paper plates
Scissors
Marker
Crayons
Glitter paint
Stickers
Self-sticking bows

WHAT YOU DO

1 Cut the centers out of the paper plates, making paper wreaths. Print "God Cares" across the top of each wreath.

2 Direct children to use the crayons, stickers, and glitter paint to decorate their wreaths.

3 Allow each child to choose a bow to stick on his or her wreath. Encourage children to think of a place to hang their wreaths at home—on a door, a doorknob, or a wall.

WHAT YOU TALK ABOUT
Tell me about where you live.
Where will you hang your wreath to help you remember that God cares.

Surprise House

WHAT YOU NEED

Construction paper
Glue
Scissors
Marker
Stickers of children
House pattern from page 142

WHAT YOU DO

1. Cut houses out of construction paper. Make window flaps on the houses by cutting on the solid lines and folding on the dotted lines. You may want to reinforce the flaps by adding transparent tape at the folds. Print "God Gives Us Houses" above the door.

2. Help children glue their houses on plain sheets of construction paper of a contrasting color. Give each child four stickers of children to place behind the door and windows of the house.

WHAT YOU TALK ABOUT

Who gave Abraham a home?
What is in your home?
Say, "Thank You, God, for my home."

God Gives Us Houses

Our Best Friend Hearts

WHAT YOU NEED

Red construction paper
White paper
Scissors
White yarn
Black marker
Hole punch
Heart pattern from page 153 and
    Jesus pattern from page 127

WHAT YOU DO

1. Cut out two hearts from red construction paper for each child. Punch holes in the heart where indicated on the pattern. Do two hearts together so they will match. In one of each pair of hearts, cut a 3" slot about 2" from the point of the heart. This will be a pocket when the hearts are sewn together by the children.

2. Photocopy and cut out a Jesus picture for each child. Cut yarn into 36" lengths, one piece per child. Dip the ends of the yarn in white glue, twist to a point, and let dry.

3. Give each child a pair of hearts and a piece of yarn. Help the children feed the yarn through the holes to sew the hearts together. When the sewing is completed, tie a bow with the leftover yarn. Then let each child slip a picture of Jesus into the pocket on the heart.

WHAT YOU TALK ABOUT

Who are your friends?
Who is our best friend?
Point to our best friend on your heart.

Bible words Puzzle

WHAT YOU NEED

4" x 12" rectangles of poster board
Construction paper
Marker
Glue
Oval, star, heart, and house patterns
    from page 150

WHAT YOU DO

1. Trace the four patterns onto each poster board rectangle and add the word "at" as shown in the illustration. Also cut ovals, stars, hearts, and houses each from a different color of construction paper. Print the words onto the separate pieces as shown in the illustration.

2. Let children choose the appropriate shapes and glue them onto their poster board rectangle.

WHAT YOU TALK ABOUT

What do the words on our posters say?
How will you help at home?

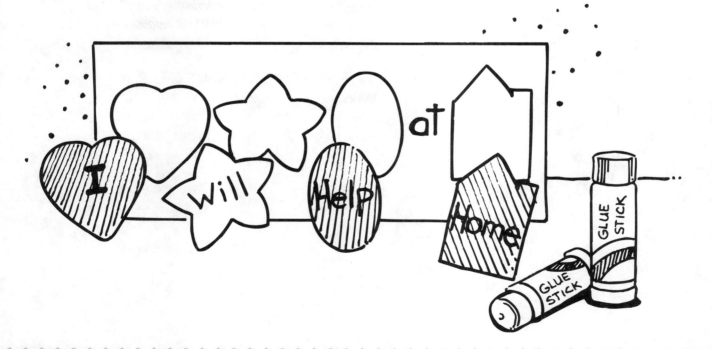

Flying Birds

WHAT YOU NEED
Many colors of construction paper
Yarn
White glue
Hole punch
Bird and wings patterns from page
128

WHAT YOU DO

1. Cut out one bird and one pair of wings from construction paper for each child in your class.

2. Punch a hole near the center of the bird and cut slits where indicated on the pattern. Cut yarn into 15" lengths.

3. Give children the birds, wings, and yarn. Help them insert the wings into the slits on the birds.

4. Help children tie the yarn through the holes in the bird. Show them how to fly their birds around the room.

WHAT YOU TALK ABOUT
Where do you see birds go?
Where are some places you like to go?
Where does God care for birds and for you?

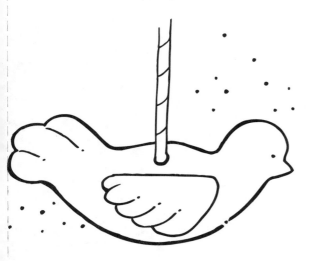

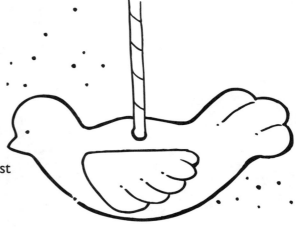

WANT TO DO MORE?
Bring in a tree branch and set it upright in a coffee can filled with gravel or dirt. After the children "fly" their birds, let them nest them in the tree branches for the rest of your time together.

Joseph Puppet

WHAT YOU NEED
Tagboard
Marker
Craft sticks
Fabric scraps
Glue or tape
Puppet pattern from page 150

WHAT YOU DO

1. Cut puppet figures from tagboard. Add faces with marker. Cut fabric scraps for clothes.

2. Have children glue or tape the puppets to the craft sticks and add the fabric clothes.

WHAT YOU TALK ABOUT
Who did Joseph help in our Bible story?
Who can you help?

My Family Place Mat

WHAT YOU NEED

Construction paper
Picture of the children's families
    (or pictures of families cut from
    magazines)
Clear, adhesive-backed plastic
Glue
Marker

WHAT YOU DO

1. Print "My Family Loves Me" on the construction paper. Cut clear, adhesive-backed plastic into 13" x 10" pieces. You will need one sheet of construction paper and two sheets of plastic for each child.

2. Guide children to color their construction paper mats and glue pictures of their families or pictures of families from magazines onto their mats. Cover both sides of the mats with clear, adhesive-backed plastic to waterproof them.

WHAT YOU TALK ABOUT

Who is in your family?
Who gave you a family to love you?

25

Helping Hats

WHAT YOU NEED
Red and blue paper plates
White paper
Red and blue crayons
Scissors
Glue
Safety pins
Fire and police badge patterns from page 127

WHAT YOU DO

1. Cut the paper plates in half. Then cut the inner circle of the plate out, making a visor. Use a paper hole punch to punch holes in either end of the hat. Then thread a piece of string through the holes and tie together to fit the hats to the children's heads. Photocopy and cut out fire and police badges.

2. Have children choose to be a fireman or a policeman. Give each child the appropriate colored hat and two badges. They may scribble color the badges. Help them glue one badge to their hat. Pin the other badge to their shirt.

WHAT YOU TALK ABOUT
What helper are you? Who gives us helpers? What other helpers has God given us?

cut out center

cut in half

clocks

WHAT YOU NEED

Paper plates
Black construction paper
Paper fasteners
Black marker
Magazine pictures representing
  what children do throughout the
  day—beds, toys, food, other boys
  and girls (friends), playground
  equipment, vehicles, and so on
Glue
Clock hands patterns from page
  128

WHAT YOU DO

1. Cut clock hands from black construction paper for each child. Print clock numbers on the paper plates.

2. Give children the clocks and ask them to choose pictures of things they do each day to glue on the clock.

3. Help children push the paper fasteners through the clock hands and face. Show the children how to move the clock hands to point to different numbers and pictures.

WHAT YOU TALK ABOUT

Point your clock to a picture of a time God
  cares for you.
Tell about your picture.

Squirrels

WHAT YOU NEED

Brown, gray, and black construction
    paper
Empty peanut shells
Glue
Scissors
Squirrel pattern from page 127

WHAT YOU DO

1. Cut out a gray squirrel for each child. Cut a large hole in a sheet of brown construction paper for each child.

2. Show children how to glue the brown papers over sheets of black construction paper to make the squirrel's home.

3. Guide children to glue peanut shells for the squirrel's food. Show them how to move their squirrels in and out of the home.

WHAT YOU TALK ABOUT

What home did God give the squirrel?
What home did God give you?
What did God give the squirrel to eat?
What does God give you to eat?

28

water Cup

WHAT YOU NEED

Paper drinking cups
Scissors
Blue crayons
Fish and sea creature stickers
Glue

WHAT YOU DO

1. Cut around half of the paper drinking cups about halfway down, making a wavy edge. See the illustration.

2. Guide children to color the wavy cups blue. Then put glue inside the cups and help them glue full-size cups inside the wavy cups. Let them decorate their cups with stickers and crayons.

WHAT YOU TALK ABOUT

Where did the people in the Bible story get water?
Where do you get your water?
When you drink from your cup, say, "Thank You, God, for water."

cut here

Giving Poster

WHAT YOU NEED
7" x 11" pieces of poster board
Craft sticks
Discarded jewelry
Rickrack or braid scraps
Scissors or pinking shears
Fabric scraps
Tape
Glue
Pennies

WHAT YOU DO

1. At the top of the poster board, print "God's people give." About two thirds of the way down, print "I give at church." Glue a piece of rickrack or braid across the board just above the lower words. See the illustration. Cut fabric scraps into small squares, using pinking shears if possible.

2. Guide children to choose pieces of fabric and jewelry to glue or tape to the top of the poster. Then give children one or two pennies to tape on the lower part of the poster.

WHAT YOU TALK ABOUT
What did God's people give to God?
What will you give at church?

worship Foldout

WHAT YOU NEED

9" squares of construction paper
Crayons
Scissors
Marker
Glue
Worship pictures from page 151

1 ## WHAT YOU DO

Fold the construction paper squares as shown in the illustration. You should have a square with four flaps to open. Print "I worship God" on the outside of the flaps as shown. Photocopy and cut out the worship pictures.

2 Let children color their foldouts and worship pictures. Then guide them to glue one picture beneath each flap of their worship foldouts.

WHAT YOU TALK ABOUT

How did Joshua show he loved God?
How can you show your love for God?
Lift the flaps on your foldout to find the worship pictures.

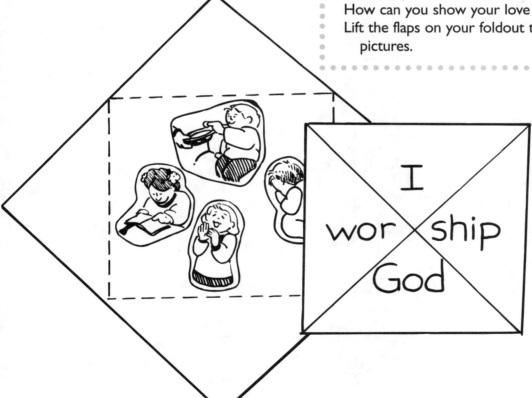

Paper Doll Friends

WHAT YOU NEED
Construction paper
Glue
Crayons
Fabric scraps
Doll pattern from page 151

WHAT YOU DO

1 Fold each sheet of construction paper into three equal parts. Using the pattern, cut paper dolls from folded paper, making sure you do not cut through hands. Do not unfold. Cut fabric scraps for clothing for the dolls. Print "I will help" on sheets of construction paper.

2 Help children unfold their dolls and glue them to the construction paper. Then let them color the dolls and choose clothing to glue on their dolls.

WHAT YOU TALK ABOUT
Who was in Ruth's family in our story?
Who is in your family?
How can you help your family?

Thank-You Card

WHAT YOU NEED
Construction paper
Pastel shades of tissue paper
Marker
Crayons
Flower patterns from page 140

WHAT YOU DO

1. Fold sheets of construction paper in half. Scallop one edge 2" down from the top. See the illustration. Print the word "Mother" (or whatever word your children are more likely to use) immediately below the scalloped edge. On the inside of the cards, print "Thank you, Mother, for all you do" on the bottom half of the paper. Cut flowers out of tissue paper.

2. Guide children to choose flowers to glue to the upper half of the inside of their cards. Help them use crayons to add stems to the flowers and to decorate their cards.

WHAT YOU TALK ABOUT
Who gave us mothers to love us?
What will you say to your mother when you give her your card?

Personalized T-shirt

WHAT YOU NEED
Construction paper
Felt or fabric for letters or pre-cut
  letters
Scissors
Glue
Marker
Crayons
T-shirt pattern from page 143

WHAT YOU DO

1 Cut t-shirts from construction paper. Print "God gives us clothes" on the bottoms of the shirts. Cut letters out of fabric for the names of the children.

2 Let children decorate their shirts with crayons. As they work, cut out any additional letters for names of visitors.

3 Help children glue the letters on their shirts. Put a small dot of glue on each letter and hand the letters, one at a time, to each child.

WHAT YOU TALK ABOUT
Who brought clothes for Samuel in our Bible story?
What clothes do you have?
Say, "Thank You, God, for clothes."

Church Helper Necklace

WHAT YOU NEED
4" circles of poster board
24"-26" lengths of yarn
Glue
Marker
Plastic drinking straws
Hole punch
Pendant patterns from page 151

WHAT YOU DO

1. Photocopy and cut out the pendants. Dip the ends of the yarn in glue and allow them to dry. Cut straws into various lengths.

2. Help children glue the pendant to the poster board circle. Then punch two holes in the top of each pendant.

3. Guide children to string the pendants onto the yarn and then add several pieces of plastic straw on each side to form a necklace. Tie at an appropriate length for each child's neck.

WHAT YOU TALK ABOUT
Who helped in the temple-church in our story?
How will you help at church?

key Chain

WHAT YOU NEED

Cardboard or lightweight poster
  board
Chenille wire (or key chains)
Stapler
Crayons
Fun stickers
Key tag pattern from page 140

WHAT YOU DO

1. Cut key tags out of cardboard or poster board. Fold down the flap at the top of the tag and staple. Make sure the staples are tight and flat.

2. Give children 6" pieces of chenille wire to push through the top of their key tags. Help them fasten the wire together to form a loop.

3. Guide children to color the key chains. Allow them to choose several stickers to decorate their chains.

WHAT YOU TALK ABOUT

Who gave us daddies?
What will you say to your daddy when you give him his key chain?

Thumbprint Plaque

WHAT YOU NEED
Craft sticks
Ink pad
Marker
Glue
Paper

WHAT YOU DO

1. Cut 4¼" squares of paper. Print the Bible words "God is love. 1 John 4:8" on the paper.

2. Help the children glue four craft sticks together to make a frame. (If you have very young children, glue the frames together before the craft.) Allow several minutes for the glue to dry.

3. Guide the children to put their thumbs on the ink pad and then make prints on the white squares.

4. Put glue around the frames and let the children place their papers on the glue.

WHAT YOU TALK ABOUT
What do the Bible words on the plaque say?
What friends did God give you to love you?
What friend could you give your plaque to?

Helping Plate

WHAT YOU NEED
Paper plates
Crayons
Marker
Yarn
Hole punch
Helping stickers (optional)

WHAT YOU DO

1 Print "I am big enough to HELP" on the plates as shown in the illustration. Punch a hole in the top of each plate and string yarn through the hole for a hanger.

2 Trace each child's hands in the center of the plate. Guide children to color their plates and decorate them with helping stickers, if available.

WHAT YOU TALK ABOUT
Who helped his friend Mephibosheth in our Bible story?
How will you help a friend?

Prayer Spinner

WHAT YOU NEED

Two colors of poster board
Glue
Paper fasteners
Pictures of things children can
 pray for or thank God
 for—families, pictures from
 God's world, a sick person,
 and so on
Arrow pattern from page 144

WHAT YOU DO

1. Cut out 8" circles of poster board. Cut arrows from the second color of poster board. Use a pin or tip of a pair of scissors to put small holes in the center of the circles and in the ends of the arrows.

2. Let children choose pictures of things they can pray for and glue the pictures around the edges of the circles. Give a paper fastener to one child at a time and help her put it in the hole in the arrow and then into the hole in the circle. Let her spread the ends on the back of the circle.

WHAT YOU TALK ABOUT

Point your arrow to something you can pray about. What will you say to God?

Corn on the Cob

WHAT YOU NEED

Green and yellow construction
   paper
White paper
Glue
1" wide paintbrush
Marker
Corn husk pattern from page 143

WHAT YOU DO

1. Cut yellow construction paper into 1" squares (like mosaic tiles). Cut green husks using the pattern. Print the words "God gives us food" on the husks. Draw a corn-cob shape, about 2" wide x 8" long on the white paper. See the illustration.

2. Give the children the white paper with the corn cob shapes. Paint glue in the corn cob on each child's paper. Then let children place the yellow squares in the corn cob shape.

3. Show children how to glue the husks over the corn cobs.

WHAT YOU TALK ABOUT

What food did God send Elijah?
What food that God gives us is in our pictures?
What other foods that God gave us do you like?

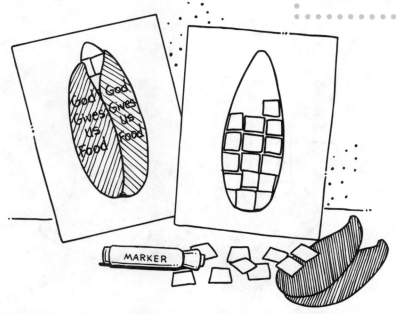

Balloon Reminder

WHAT YOU NEED
Balloons
Wide-tip permanent marker
Stickers
String

WHAT YOU DO

1. Blow up balloons and tie 12"-18" strings on balloons. Carefully print "Share" in large letters on each balloon.

2. Allow children to decorate their balloons with stickers.

WHAT YOU TALK ABOUT
Who shared with Elijah in our story?
What will you share with a friend?

Elisha's Room

WHAT YOU NEED

7" x 4½" pieces of brown
    construction paper
4" x 2½" pieces of brown
    construction paper
Yellow construction paper
Glue
Marker
Crayons

WHAT YOU DO

1. In each larger piece of brown construction paper, cut a door about 1¼" x 2½" in size. See the illustration. Leave a hinge on one side. Cut a small window, 1" x 1" from the smaller rectangle of construction paper. On the yellow paper, print "Share at home."

2. Guide the children to glue their large rectangles onto the yellow construction paper. Show them how to open their doors. Then have them glue the smaller rectangle onto the tops of their houses to make "Elisha's room."

WHAT YOU TALK ABOUT

Who shared with Elisha in our story?
What could you share at your home?

Naaman Puppet

WHAT YOU NEED
Styrofoam cups
Scissors
Craft sticks
Glue
Crayons
Naaman pattern from page 127

WHAT TO DO

1 Cut out a Naaman figure for each child. Cut a small slit in the bottom of each paper cup.

2 Guide children to color Naaman and their cups.

3 Show the children how to glue Naaman to one end of the craft stick and stick the craft stick down through the slit on the bottom of their cup. They should be able to push Naaman up and down in the cup, using the craft stick.

WHAT YOU TALK ABOUT
How did God take care of Naaman?
Tell about a time you were sick.
How did God take care of you?

Bible Bookmark

WHAT YOU NEED

2" x 6" strips of poster board or
  construction paper
8" lengths of yarn
Hole punch
Bible and Jesus stickers
Crayons
Marker

WHAT YOU DO

1 Punch a hole in the top of each strip of poster board. Print the words "We love Him" on each strip.

2 Guide children to put Bible and Jesus stickers on their bookmarks. Allow them to decorate the bookmarks with crayons.

3 Help children double their yarn, put the loop through the holes, then pull both ends through the loop and pull tight.

WHAT YOU TALK ABOUT

Who read God's word in our Bible story?
Who can read the Bible to you?
Where will you put your bookmark to help you remember to read the Bible?

Helping Fan

WHAT YOU NEED

Poster board
Craft stick
Stickers
Crayons
Marker
Glue
Fan pattern from page 152

WHAT YOU DO

1. Cut fans from poster board, using the pattern on page 152. Cut two per child.

2. Help the children put their two fans together with a craft stick in between. Let children decorate their fans with stickers and crayons.

WHAT YOU TALK ABOUT

Who helped take care of the church in our Bible story?

What can you share to help take care of our church?

Singing Shaker

WHAT YOU NEED
Small plastic containers with lids
   that can be glued shut (small
   drink containers, margarine tubs)
Glue
Stickers
Labels
Marker
Dry beans or rice

WHAT YOU DO

1. Print "We love Him" on the labels. Remove labels from containers or cover them with clear, adhesive-backed plastic.

2. Guide children to put a handful of beans or rice in their containers and help them glue the lid shut.

3. Help each child put a Bible words label on the container. Let children decorate their shakers with stickers.

WHAT YOU TALK ABOUT
Who sang to God in our story?
What songs do we sing to God?
Let's use our shakers to sing to God.

Liter Liter Bottle

WHAT YOU NEED

One- or two-liter size plastic
  bottles
Scissors
Labels
Stickers
Yarn

WHAT YOU DO

1. Cut a hole about 3" or 4" in diameter in the bottles, leaving the necks of the bottles intact. On plain labels, print the words "Help keep God's world clean."

2. Guide children to put the labels on the bottles. Help them put yarn through the two openings in the bottle and tie to make a handle. See the illustration. Children can decorate their bottles with stickers.

WHAT YOU TALK ABOUT

What did Nehemiah and the people help build in our story?
How can you use your litter bottle to help?

Bible Wall Hanging

WHAT YOU NEED

Felt or burlap
Black felt
Craft sticks
Red yarn and another color of yarn
Permanent marker
Glue
Scissors

WHAT YOU DO

1. Notch the craft sticks about ⅜" from each end. Cut the felt or burlap into 3" x 6" pieces, one for each child. Turn down 1" of the material and glue to make a pocket for the craft sticks.

2. Cut 1" x 1½" pieces of black felt. Cut 3" pieces of any color of yarn and 1" pieces of red yarn. Glue one piece of red yarn to the right side of each piece of black felt, leaving an end of the yarn hanging below the felt. See the illustration. Print the words "Love God" on the large pieces of cloth.

3. Help children glue their Bibles on the hangings, yarn side down. Then help them slip the craft sticks into the pockets and tie the yarn hangers on both ends of the sticks, at the notches.

WHAT YOU TALK ABOUT

What is the book on your hanging?
Who does the Bible teach us about?

48

Body Puzzle

WHAT YOU NEED

Butcher paper or other large
    sheets of paper
Crayons
Scissors
Rubber bands

WHAT YOU DO

1. Cut paper in lengths that will be long enough for children to lie down on. On each piece print "God made me."

2. Have children lie down on pieces of paper while you trace around their bodies with crayon. Then let the children color their pictures to match their hair and clothing.

3. Cut the bodies into pieces to make puzzles. Label each child's puzzle pieces. Allow children to put their puzzles together. Then roll up the puzzles and hold together with rubber bands.

WHAT YOU TALK ABOUT

Show me what you can do with your arms? Legs? Hands? Feet?
Who made your arms, legs, hands, and feet?

Five-Senses Tray

WHAT YOU NEED

Styrofoam meat or vegetable trays
Tape
Glue
Small bells
Chenille wire
Raisins or wrapped candy
Cotton balls
Perfume or lemon juice
Rocks, pine cones, pieces of velvet, sandpaper

WHAT YOU DO

1. Print "God Made Our Senses" on the trays. Cut chenille wire in very short pieces. Punch two small holes in each tray, about ¾" apart. Bend the chenille wire in half and push an end of the wire through the holes in a bell. Now push the ends of the wire through the two holes in the tray and twist the wire securely on the back of the tray.

2. Help the children glue or tape the other items on the tray. Place a few drops of the perfume or lemon juice on the cotton balls, sandpaper, or velvet. Encourage the children to see, touch, smell, hear, and taste.

WHAT YOU TALK ABOUT

What do you like to see? Touch? Smell? Hear? Taste? Who made you able to see, touch, smell, hear, and taste?

Feelings Frame

WHAT YOU NEED
Paper plates
Crayons
Paper towel rolls, one-half for each
    child
Marker

WHAT YOU DO

1. Cut five-inch circles out of the middle of each plate, and cut a 1" slit at an angle in each paper towel roll. See the illustration. Print "God Made My Feelings" on the plates.

2. Let children decorate the plates and rolls with crayons. Then help them insert the plates in the slits in the paper towel rolls. Show them how to hold the frame in front of their faces as they show their feelings.

WHAT YOU TALK ABOUT
Show me how you feel when you are sleepy. Hungry. Hugging your mom. Eating peas. Playing with toys Mad. Get hurt.
Who made you able to feel sad, happy, and tired?

"God Made Me" Pennant

WHAT YOU NEED

Construction paper
Drinking straws
Marker
Crayons
Items to decorate the pennants,
    such as stickers and glitter paint
Hole punch

WHAT YOU DO

1. Cut out the triangular-shaped pennants. Punch holes for the straws as shown. On one side of the pennants print "God made . . ."

2. Give each child a pennant. Print their name on the blank side of the pennant and guide them to draw a picture of themselves. Then allow them to decorate their pennants, using stickers and glitter paint.

3. Help each child put a straw through the holes in the pennant.

WHAT YOU TALK ABOUT

Who made you?
What do you like about you?
Let's wave our pennants and sing a song to thank God for making us. (Choose a favorite praise song of the children.)

WANT TO DO MORE?

Ask parents several weeks ahead of time to send in a picture of their children to use on the pennant. Or bring an instant camera and take pictures of the children to use on the pennants.

Lion Pizzas

WHAT YOU NEED

Small pizza crusts (pitas, pizza
   rounds found in Lunchables,
   halves of burger buns)
Spreadable cream cheese
Grated cheese
Radish or carrot slices, cut into
   triangles
Sliced black olives
Plastic knives

WHAT YOU DO

1. Help children spread cream cheese on their crusts.
Then guide them to use olives to make the lions'
eyes and a slice of carrot or radish for the noses.
Show them how to sprinkle grated cheese around
the edges to make the manes.

WHAT YOU TALK ABOUT

Who in our story talked to God every day?
When will you talk to God during the day?
Let's talk to God before we eat our lion pizzas.

Good-News Letters

WHAT YOU NEED
Construction paper
Crayons
Glue
Marker
Stickers
Letter and pictures from page 129

WHAT YOU DO

1. Photocopy and cut out the letter and pictures.

2. Make envelopes by folding sheets of construction paper crosswise, leaving 1½" at the tops to make flaps. Help the children glue the sides of the envelopes. Set aside to dry.

3. Help the children glue the letters and pictures to construction paper. Guide them to use crayons to decorate their letters. Print the appropriate names in the blanks on each child's letter.

4. Fold the letters in quarters and insert in the envelopes. Use stickers to hold the envelopes shut. Encourage parents to help the children deliver the letters to their friends.

WHAT YOU TALK ABOUT
What good news do your letters tell?
Who will you give your letter to?
What will you tell that friend about Jesus?

Angel Ornament

WHAT YOU NEED

6 oz. Styrofoam cups
10" yellow chenille wires
Gold poster board
1" lengths of red yarn (1 per child)
6" lengths of gold yarn (6 per child)
2" Styrofoam balls
Gold glitter in salt shakers
Glue
Newspaper
Angel wings pattern from page 145

WHAT YOU DO

1. Twist a large knot in one end of the chenille wire and insert through the bottom of a cup so the knot is inside the cup. Pull up tight. Push wire through the Styrofoam ball to form the head of an angel. Twist the wire in a circle to form the halo above the head, then use the rest of the wire to make a hook for hanging the ornament. Make an angel for each child in your group.

2. Cut wings from gold poster board. Print, "God sent His Son" on the backs of the wings.

3. Cover the work area with newspaper. Put glue around the edge of each wing and down the front of the cup angel and let children sprinkle glitter on the wet glue. Put dabs of glue on for eyes and mouth and let the children add the red yarn for the mouth and glitter for the eyes.

4. Glue the wings to the back of the angel. Have the children put their hands inside the cup and press down and hold the wings in place for a few minutes until they dry.

5. Spread glue on the top of the angels' heads and show children how to add gold yarn hair.

WHAT YOU TALK ABOUT

What was the happy news the angel told Mary?
Who was the baby boy that Mary would have?

star Chain Decoration

WHAT YOU NEED

Yellow, red, and green construction
    paper
Christmas stickers
Glue
Tape
White paper
Star pattern from page 138

WHAT YOU DO

1 Enlarge the patterns and cut stars from yellow paper.
Cut 1" x 5" strips from the red and green paper.
Print the following poem on each star.

> Little star, shining bright,
> How many days 'till Christmas night?
> Jesus' birthday will soon be here.
> Thank You, God, for Your Son so dear.

2 Help children make chains of the red and green
strips. Give children a strip for each day until
Christmas.

3 Guide children to decorate their stars with
Christmas stickers. Then tape the chain securely to
the star.

WHAT YOU TALK ABOUT

Take a circle from your chain each day until
    Christmas day.
Say, "Thank You, God, for baby Jesus."

Baby Jesus Picture

WHAT YOU NEED
Brown, white, and blue
  construction paper
Scissors
Glue
2" x 3" pieces of flannel or other
  soft cloth
Straw, hay, raffia, or raveled burlap
Crayons
Manger and baby patterns from
  page 130

WHAT YOU DO

1. Cut a manger out of brown paper and a baby Jesus out of white paper for each child.

2. Give children blue construction paper and guide them to glue the manger and baby to the paper. Let them color the pictures.

3. Help children glue a piece of flannel over baby Jesus and glue hay in the manger.

WHAT YOU TALK ABOUT
Who is the special baby?
Where is the baby sleeping?

WANT TO DO MORE?
Do the following finger play with the children.
"A stable, *(Tent hands.)*
A manger, *(Cup hands and hold together to form a bed.)*
A baby. *(Rock arms back and forth as though holding a baby.)*
Shh! *(Place finger to lips.)* The baby's sleeping.
Let's be very quiet and not say a word."

Trumpets

WHAT YOU NEED

Styrofoam cups
X-acto knife
Glitter
Glue
Newspaper

WHAT YOU DO

1. Cut the bottoms out of the cups with an X-acto knife or other sharp instrument.

2. Cover the table with newspaper for easy clean up. Give each child a cup. Show the children how to spread glue over the outside of the cup, then sprinkle it with glitter.

WHAT YOU TALK ABOUT

What good news did the angels tell the shepherds? Let's shout our good news through our trumpets.

GLUE

Glitter   Glitter

Handprint sheep

WHAT YOU NEED

Black construction paper
Scissors
Cotton balls
11" lengths of bright-colored yarn
Glue
Silver or white colored pencil

WHAT YOU DO

1 Draw around each child's hand on a piece of black paper and cut out the handprint. Mark an eye with a white or silver pencil. (Since making the handprints takes time, you may wish to trace and cut out each child's handprint the week before this activity.)

2 Show children how to glue cotton balls to their sheep, leaving the faces and hooves black. Help them tie yarn bows around the necks of their sheep. The children can help you with the bows by holding their fingers on the knot as you tie.

WHAT YOU TALK ABOUT

Who took care of sheep in our story?
Who told the shepherds some happy news?
What happy news did the angels tell the shepherds?

Christmas surprise Rubbings

WHAT YOU NEED

Construction paper
White paper
Cardboard
Scissors
Crayons
Sheep, baby, star, and angel patterns
from page 138

WHAT YOU DO

1 Cut out cardboard patterns, using the shapes listed above. Make a pattern for each child. Glue the patterns to construction paper

2 Place a piece of white paper over each pattern. Guide children to scribble color the white paper all over. As they color, the shapes beneath the paper should show up. Allow children to trade and try different patterns if they finish their first picture.

WHAT YOU TALK ABOUT

What surprise picture did you find when you colored? Who saw a surprise in the temple? What was the surprise?

star Viewers

WHAT YOU NEED

Construction paper
Cardboard tissue rolls (1 per child)
4" squares of blue cellophane paper
Star stickers
Rubber bands
Tape

WHAT YOU DO

① Give each child a cardboard tissue roll. Help the children cover their rolls with construction paper and fasten in place with tape.

② Have children put star stickers on the cellophane paper. Then place the paper over the end of the cardboard tube and hold in place with a rubber band. Show the children how to hold the star viewer up to the light to make the stars shine.

WHAT YOU TALK ABOUT

Who followed a star to see little Jesus?
What did the wise men give baby Jesus?

Crown

WHAT YOU NEED
Construction paper
Glitter glue
Tape
Glue
Newspaper

WHAT YOU DO

1. Cut crowns from construction paper.

2. Allow children to color their crowns and use glitter glue to make designs on their crowns. Allow the crowns to dry.

3. Tape the crowns together to fit each child's head.

WHAT YOU TALK ABOUT
Pretend you are a wise man. What will you give Jesus?
What will you say to Jesus?

Growth Chart

WHAT YOU NEED

Construction paper
Tape
Fun stickers
Marker
Ruler patterns from page 145

WHAT YOU DO

1. Cut sheets of construction paper in half. Print "I grow like Jesus grew" on the pieces of paper and draw a happy face. See the illustration. Copy the ruler strips from page 145 and cut them out. Make a set of strips for each child.

2. Help the children tape the strips together to make a 48" strip. Then tape the long strip to the construction paper piece. Allow children to decorate their strips with stickers.

3. When children are finished, mark each child's height on his chart.

WHAT YOU TALK ABOUT

What did you look like when you were a baby?
What did you do?
What can you do now that you are bigger?
You are growing just like Jesus did.

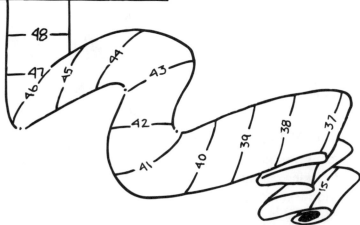

Growing Up Pictures

WHAT YOU NEED
Construction paper
Marker
Crayons
Baby pictures cut from magazines
Tape

WHAT YOU DO
1. Give each child a piece of paper and help her trace around her hand on the right side of the paper. Then allow children to color their pictures.

2. Encourage each child to choose a baby picture and glue it to the left side of the paper. Print "(Child's name) grows up like Jesus did" on each paper.

WHAT YOU TALK ABOUT
What did you do when you were a baby?
What things can you do now that you are bigger?
You are growing bigger, just like Jesus did.

WANT TO DO MORE?
Send a note home with children several weeks before the craft, asking parents to send in baby pictures. Be sure to provide some magazine baby pictures for children visitors or children who do not have a picture.

Obey Chart

WHAT YOU NEED

Construction paper
White paper
Paper fasteners
Arrow pattern and pictures from
    page 144

WHAT YOU DO

1. Print "I will obey like Jesus did" on pieces of light-colored construction paper. Copy and cut out the pictures from page 144. Cut arrows from dark shades of paper.

2. Guide children to glue the pictures around the paper. Then help children put paper fasteners through the arrow and attach it to the center of the paper.

WHAT YOU TALK ABOUT

Point your arrow to a picture.
How can you obey?
You are obeying like Jesus did.

stick Puppets

WHAT YOU NEED
Construction paper
Craft sticks
Faces of children cut from catalogs
  or magazines
Glue sticks
Crayons
Tape
Marker
Puppet pattern from page 133

WHAT YOU DO
1 Cut puppet bodies out of construction paper. Print "Come to church" on the craft sticks.

2 Help the children choose faces to glue on their puppets and color their puppets. Then help them tape craft sticks to the back of the puppets.

WHAT YOU TALK ABOUT
How did Andrew help Peter learn about Jesus?
Who could you invite to learn about Jesus?
Use your puppet and pretend to invite your friend
  to church.

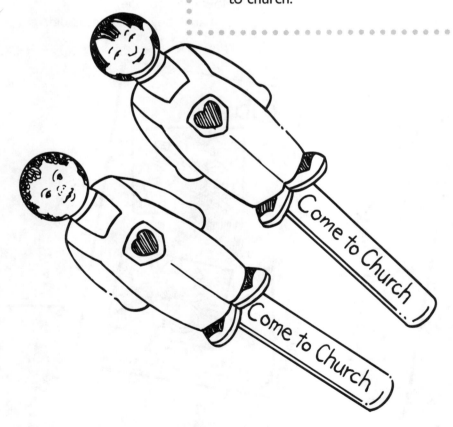

Prayer Basket

WHAT YOU NEED

Construction paper
White paper
Marker
Tape
Crayons
Stickers

WHAT YOU DO

1 Cut 6" x 7" pieces of construction paper. Fold up 1½" on the edges as shown in the illustration and cut where indicated. Fold the ends and glue. On one end of each basket, print "We talk to Jesus." Cut 1" x 7" strips of paper for the handles. Cut the white paper into small squares that will fit in the baskets.

2 Let children decorate their baskets with crayons and stickers. Help them name things they can talk to Jesus about. They can draw pictures of those things on the paper squares, or you can print their responses on the squares. Help them put the squares in their baskets and tape handles to the baskets.

WHAT YOU TALK ABOUT

Who talked to Jesus in our story?
What will you say to Jesus?

cut
← solid lines →

We Talk To
☺ Jesus

"Friend of Jesus" Viewfinder

WHAT YOU NEED
Cardboard tubes
Construction paper
Crayons
Fun stickers
Glue or tape

WHAT YOU DO
1. Cut the construction paper to fit the cardboard tubes. Print "Find a friend of Jesus" at one end of the paper.

2. Let children decorate the papers with stickers and crayons. Then help them glue or tape the papers around the cardboard tubes. Show them how to use their tubes to find friends of Jesus.

WHAT YOU TALK ABOUT
Who was Jesus a friend to in the story?
Look through your tube to find a friend of Jesus.

Boy Puppet

WHAT YOU NEED
Construction paper
Scissors
Crayons
Brads
Boy patterns from page 129

WHAT YOU DO

1. Photocopy and cut out the top and bottom parts of the boy for each child.

2. Give children the patterns and allow them to color the boy.

3. Help children push a brad through the torso and legs of the boy to fasten them together. Show children how to make the boy lie down as though sick, and then sit up as though well again.

WHAT YOU TALK ABOUT
Use your puppet to show me how the boy felt before Jesus helped him.
How did the boy look after Jesus made Him well?
Jesus is the Son of God. Only Jesus could make a sick boy well.

Envelope Bible

WHAT YOU NEED
Small white envelopes
Bible
Address-size labels
Glue
Marker
Bible words cards from page 134

WHAT YOU DO

1 Print "Holy Bible" on the labels. Make copies of the Bible words cards.

2 Show the children the Bible. Help them position their labels on their envelopes to make them look like the front of the Bible. Give each child the Bible words cards and help them put the cards in the envelopes.

WHAT YOU TALK ABOUT
Where are the words on our cards from?
We can listen and learn from Bible words. (Help children find each card and say the words after you "Love God." "We pray to God." "Love each other.")

HOLY BIBLE

Linda Smith

OVE OD

Mark 12:30

VE AY O D

13:7

VE CH ER

15:17

ians

Fishermen Boats

WHAT YOU NEED
Paper plates
Empty netted potato sacks
Stapler
Glue
Goldfish crackers
Crayons

WHAT YOU DO

1. Fold the paper plates in half. Cut strips of netted potato sacks for the fish nets.

2. Allow children to color their paper plate boats. Drape a net on the side of each boat and staple it as shown in the illustration. Give children some goldfish to put in their nets. Show children how to rock their boats back and forth.

WHAT YOU TALK ABOUT
Who was a friend to four fishermen in our story? What did Jesus help his friends catch in their nets?

Jesus Helps His Friends Catch Fish (Luke 5)

seashore plaque

WHAT YOU NEED
Styrofoam meat trays
Green or deep blue construction
    paper
Fish stickers
Sand or cornmeal
Small seashells
Glue
8" lengths of yarn
Paintbrushes
Waves pattern from page 145

WHAT YOU DO

1 Cut construction paper waves from the pattern. Print "Jesus is the Son of God" on the trays.

2 Put glue on the meat trays and show children how to spread the glue over the lower part of the tray using a paintbrush. Help them glue the waves onto tray.

3 Put glue on the lower part of the waves and help children sprinkle sand or cornmeal on the glue. Shake off the excess into a pan or box. Put dabs of glue in the sand and let children add seashells.

4 Let children put fish stickers on their waves. Tape a piece of yarn to the back of the plaque for a hanger.

WHAT YOU TALK ABOUT
Who helped Peter and his friends catch fish?
Only Jesus could help His friends catch fish because He is the Son of God.

Get-well Cards

WHAT YOU NEED

Construction paper
Pictures cut from old greeting cards
or pictures of flowers cut from
seed catalogs and magazines
Glue
Marker
Crayons

WHAT YOU DO

1. Fold sheets of construction paper in half and print "Get well soon. I will pray for you" on the inside of each card.

2. Give children the cards. Direct them to choose a picture to glue to the front of the cards. Encourage children to color their cards.

3. Print each child's name on the inside of his card. Collect the cards to give to someone who is sick. Or ask parents to help children deliver the cards to someone they know who is sick.

WHAT YOU TALK ABOUT

Who was sick in the Bible story?
Who helped the sick woman?
Jesus is the Son of God. Only Jesus could make a sick woman well.

Get Well Soon.

I Will Pray For You. ANDY

GLUE

Legs Picture

WHAT YOU NEED
Construction paper
White paper
Glue
Scissors
Crayons
Marker
Child and legs patterns from page
    146

WHAT YOU DO

1. Print "Thank You, God, for my legs" and "I can" on pieces of construction paper. Cut two slits in each paper, 3¼" long. See the illustration. Copy and cut out the patterns from page 146. Cut 3" x 12" strips of paper.

2. Show children how to glue the child's upper body into place above the slits. Then have them glue the three sets of legs on the strips of paper. Help each child slide his strip through the slits. Show him how he can make his child stand, walk, and kneel. Allow children to color their pictures.

WHAT YOU TALK ABOUT
Show me how you walk, sit, kneel, hop, and stand.
Who made a man walk in today's story?
Only Jesus could make a sick man walk because He
    is the Son of God.

Sad or Glad Face

WHAT YOU NEED

Construction paper
Black or brown yarn
Buttons for eyes and noses
Plasti-tak
Red felt
Rough fabric such as burlap
Markers
Face patterns from page 147

WHAT YOU DO

1. Trace the Matthew face pattern onto construction paper. Add outlines for the hair, eyes, and eyebrows. Cut yarn for hair 3" to 4" in length, 1" to 1½" for the beard, and ¾" for eyebrows. Cut felt smile and clothing from rough fabric.

2. Help children glue the hair, beards, clothes, eyebrows, eyes, and noses in place. Put Plasti-tak on the backs of the mouths and show children how Matthew can look sad or happy

WHAT YOU TALK ABOUT

Who was a friend to Matthew in the story?
Show me how Matthew looked before he found Jesus.
Show me how Matthew looked after he followed his friend Jesus.

Heart Hanging

WHAT YOU NEED
Brightly colored poster board
Sandpaper
Scissors
Glue
Crayons
Ribbon
Hole punch
Heart patterns from page 139

WHAT YOU DO

1 Cut the larger hearts out of poster board. Cut the slightly smaller hearts out of sandpaper. Print "Be kind" on the sandpaper hearts.

2 Let children color their sandpaper hearts. Then help them glue the sandpaper hearts onto the poster board heart. Punch a hole in the top of the poster board heart and tie a ribbon through the hole for a hanger.

WHAT YOU TALK ABOUT
Jesus teaches us to be kind to everyone. Who can you be kind to?
Jesus teaches us because He is the Son of God.
Hang your heart at home, so you can remember to be kind.

Soldier's Armor

WHAT YOU NEED
Poster board
Scissors
Tape
Glue
Crayons
Foil
Construction paper

WHAT YOU DO

1 Cut pieces of poster board in half to make shields. Cut 2" wide strips of poster board to make handles. Cut pieces of foil and construction paper to decorate the shields.

2 Let children color their shields and glue on pieces of foil and paper for decoration. Help the children tape the poster board strips to the back to make handles. Show children how to hold their shields in front to protect themselves.

WHAT YOU TALK ABOUT
Who did the soldier in our story go to see?
Who did the soldier want Jesus to help?
Only Jesus could heal a sick servant because He is
   the Son of God.

BACK

Bathtub Boats

WHAT YOU NEED

1" thick sponges
7" lengths of drinking straws
Construction paper
Clear, adhesive-backed plastic
Marker
Hole punch
Crayons
Boat and sail patterns from page
145

WHAT YOU DO

1 Use the pattern to cut a boat out of a sponge for each child. Make a small hole in the sponge for the straw. See the illustration. Cut sails out of construction paper. Print the words "God gives us water" on one side of each sail. Cover both sides of the sails with clear plastic to make them waterproof. Punch two holes on the long side of each sail where indicated.

2 Guide children to decorate their sails with crayons. (The wax will stick to the plastic.) Help children put the straws through the holes in the sail and then put the straws in the sponge to complete their boat.

WHAT YOU TALK ABOUT

Who was in a boat in a storm in the Bible story? Tell about a time that you saw a scary storm. Who will help you when you are scared?

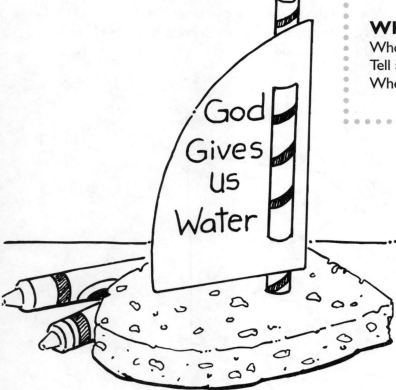

Food Baskets

WHAT YOU NEED
Construction paper
Glue sticks
Crayons
Basket, loaf, and fish patterns from
    page 131

WHAT YOU DO

1) Cut out a basket, two fish, and five loaves for each child.

2) Give children the cut-out figures and construction paper. Show children how to put glue on the outside edges only (sides and bottom) of the basket and stick it to their papers. Make sure the top of the basket is open so the loaves and fish can be put inside.

3) Encourage the children to color the basket, loaves, and fish. Then count out loud together as they put two fish and five loaves of bread in the basket.

WHAT YOU TALK ABOUT
How many loaves of bread are in your basket? How many fish?
Jesus is the Son of God. Only Jesus could feed 5,000 people with five loaves of bread and two fish.

Handprint Hanging

WHAT YOU NEED

9" squares of plain fabric (cotton or cotton blend)
12" squares of poster board
Tempera paint
Glue
Crayons and stickers
Permanent marker
Painting smocks
Materials for clean up

WHAT YOU DO

1. Print "I can pray" across the top of each fabric square. See the illustration.

2. Give children painting smocks. Allow one child at a time to place a hand in the paint and carefully lay it down on the square of material. If you have two leaders, one can print a child's name and help with the handprint while the other helps a child clean the paint from his hands and remove the smock.

3. As children complete their handprint, guide them to decorate the outer edges of the poster board squares using crayons and stickers.

4. When the paint is dry, help children glue the fabric to the poster board.

WHAT YOU TALK ABOUT

Who talked to God in our story?
What are some things you say when you talk to God?

WANT TO DO MORE?

Frame the fabric squares or use them as a pillow top, trimmed with braid glued around the edge.

Wind Chimes

WHAT YOU NEED

Lids from small margarine tubs
Yarn
Blue construction paper
Fish and sea stickers
Glue
Small seashells, six for each child
  (or large plastic soup spoons)
Hole punch

WHAT YOU DO

1. Punch 8 holes around each lid. Cut seven pieces of yarn for each child. Tie one length through two holes to make a hanger. Then tie one piece to each of the other remaining holes. Hold the circle up by the hanger and trim the rest of the yarn to one length. Cut blue circles of paper to fit the centers of the lids.

2. Guide children to glue the circles of paper in their lids and decorate them with stickers. Put a glob of glue inside each seashell and let the children put the ends of their yarn in the glue. Allow to dry.

WHAT YOU TALK ABOUT

What did Jesus do on the water in today's story?
Can you walk on water?
Only Jesus walks on water because He is the Son of God.

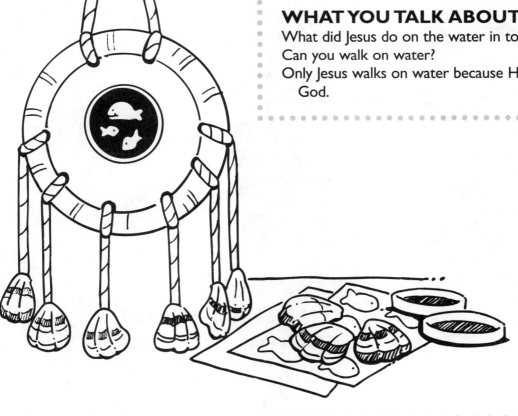

Mystery Sound Boxes

WHAT YOU NEED

Shoe boxes or other small boxes, one for each child

Glue sticks

Pictures cut from magazines of items that make sounds, such as musical instruments, animals, people, vehicles, water, and so on

Enough beans or pasta for each child to have some

Small items that make sounds when shaken, such as spoons, Lego's, cotton balls, crumpled paper, crayons, pennies, and so on

WHAT YOU DO

1. Direct children to choose pictures of items that make sounds to glue on their boxes.

2. Allow children to take turns putting different items in their boxes and shaking them to see what sound they make.

3. Give each child a handful of beans or pasta to put in their sound box to take home.

WHAT YOU TALK ABOUT

What does it mean to be "deaf"?

What did Jesus do for the deaf man in the story?

Jesus is the Son of God. Only Jesus could make a deaf man hear again.

WANT TO DO MORE?

Play a guessing game with the items you brought to put in the boxes. Help each child take a turn secretly placing an item in her box and shaking it. The other children can guess what is in the box.

Doctor Equipment

WHAT YOU NEED
Cardboard
White paper
Heavy cord
Empty thread spools
Aluminum foil
Glue sticks
Crayons
Tape

WHAT YOU DO

1. Cut cord into 36" lengths. Cut circles of cardboard 3" in diameter. Cut strips of paper 1½" wide x 22" long. Cut foil circles 3" in diameter.

2. Let the children decorate their spools with crayons. Help them put both ends of the cord through their spools. Tie a large knot in the ends of each piece of cord below the spool.

3. Help the children put glue on their cardboard circles and attach the foil circles. Then glue these to the paper strips.

4. Fit this to each child's head and fasten with tape. Show the children how to put on their doctor's gear and how to use it.

WHAT YOU TALK ABOUT
Who made the sick man in the Bible story well again?
What did the sick man tell Jesus?
What can we tell Jesus?

Helping Cup

WHAT YOU NEED

Styrofoam cups
Crayons
Stickers
Permanent marker
Large wooden or plastic beads or
　large pasta
Shoelaces or lengths of sturdy
　string

WHAT YOU DO

1　Print each child's name on a cup. Let children decorate their cups with crayons and stickers.

2　Knot each shoelace on one end. Help children count out 10 beads to put in their cups. Explain that each time they help at home, they can string a bead on their helping necklace. You may wish to provide a note to take home to parents. If you have time, let children practice stringing the helping beads on their necklaces.

WHAT YOU TALK ABOUT

Who helped a man in our story?
Who can you help at home?
How can you help?

WANT TO DO MORE?

Keep the helping cups in the classroom. Each time you see a child helping over the course of a unit of lessons or a month, add a bead to his cup. At the end of the unit, let children string the beads together to make a necklace.

My Lunch Plate

WHAT YOU NEED

Paper plates
Clear, adhesive-backed plastic
Marker
Stickers

WHAT YOU DO

1. Print the words "We eat with friends" around the edges of the plates. Also print "You are my friends. John 15:14" around the edges. Cut the clear, adhesive-backed plastic into circles large enough to cover the flat part of the plate.

2. Let the children help you apply the plastic circles to the centers of the plates. Then allow them to decorate their plates with stickers.

WHAT YOU TALK ABOUT

Who was Mary and Martha's friend in our story?
What did Jesus do with His friends?
You can talk to Jesus when you eat too!

"Come to me" Picture

WHAT YOU NEED
Construction paper
Glue
Fabric scraps
Cotton balls
Craft sticks
Crayons
Jesus and children patterns from
    page 148

WHAT YOU DO

1. Copy and cut out the figures of Jesus and the children from heavy paper. Glue the figure of Jesus to construction paper. Sketch a cloud in the sky. Cut a slit in the paper as shown on the sketch. Add the Bible words, "We love Him (1 John 4:9)."

2. Let children glue fabric scraps to Jesus and the children. Show them how to glue cotton balls to the clouds and craft sticks on the backs of the children figures. Then show them how to insert the handles of the figures into the slits and bring the children to Jesus.

WHAT YOU TALK ABOUT
Who in our story loved the children?
How do you think the children felt about seeing
    their friend Jesus?
Make the children in your picture come close to
    their friend Jesus.

Care Book

WHAT YOU NEED
Construction paper
18" lengths of yarn
Glue
Marker
Pictures of people who care for
children, such as Jesus, parents,
grandparents, teachers, police-
men, firemen, doctors, nurses
Hole punch

WHAT YOU DO
1 Cut the construction paper in half. Fold these pieces in half to make a booklet for each child. Print "People Who Care for Me" on the cover of each booklet. Punch two holes in each booklet on the fold.

2 Encourage children to choose pictures of people who care for them to glue in their booklets.

3 Help children put yarn through the holes in the booklet and tie it in a bow.

WHAT YOU TALK ABOUT
Who takes care of you?
What will you say to thank God for His care?

Jesus Loves Me Mirror

WHAT YOU NEED

Dinner-size paper plates
5" circles of aluminum foil
Paper hole punch
10" lengths of yarn
Marker
Glue

WHAT YOU DO

1. Print the words "Who does Jesus love?" on the outside edge of each paper plate.

2. Help children glue the foil mirrors to the centers of the plates.

3. Punch a hole in the top of each plate and help children put the yarn through the hole and tie it to make a hanger. Encourage children to hang their mirrors on a bedpost, doorknob, or dresser door knob.

WHAT YOU TALK ABOUT

Look in your mirrors. Who do you see that Jesus loves?
Name some friends that Jesus loves.

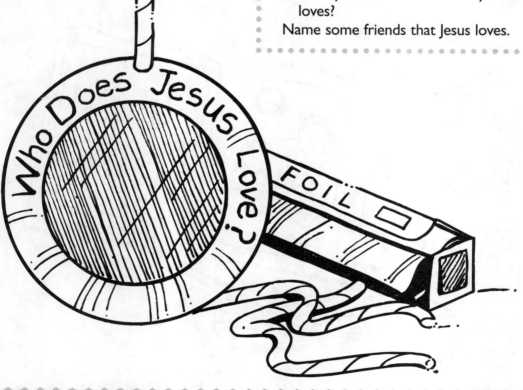

Floating Butterfly

WHAT YOU NEED

Construction paper
12" and 2" pieces of chenille wire
Scissors
Glue
Modeling clay or play dough
Butterfly pattern from page 146

WHAT YOU DO

1. Cut construction-paper butterflies. Cut circles and ovals from various colors of construction paper to glue on the butterflies.

2. Let children glue the circles and ovals on their butterflies to decorate them. Help children bend 12" chenille wires around the body of the butterflies, catching the 2" piece of chenille wire at the top to make antennae and twisting the wire at the bottom to hold it in place. See the illustration.

3. Give children pieces of clay about the size of walnuts to make bases. Show them how to roll the clay into a ball, flatten the bottom, and insert the stem of the chenille wire in the base. When the butterfly is tapped, it will seem to float in the air.

WHAT YOU TALK ABOUT

What colors do you see on your butterfly?
Who made two blind men see in our story?
Only Jesus could make blind men see because He is the Son of God.

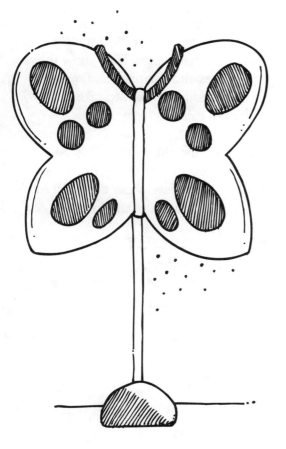

Sponge-Painted Tree

WHAT YOU NEED

Blue, brown, and white construction
  paper
Green, yellow, and orange tempera
  paint
Small pie pans
Spring-type clothespins
Newspapers
Painting smocks
Felt-tip pens
Sponges
Crayons
Glue sticks
Tree trunk and man patterns from
  page 132

WHAT YOU DO

1. Cut one Zaccheus figure from white paper and one tree trunk from brown paper for each child. Make a small slit, large enough for the Zaccheus figure where the leaf area of the tree will be. See the illustration.

2. Cover tables with newspaper. Put paint in small pie pans. Use small pieces of sponge in spring-type clothespins in place of paint brushes. Put several of these in each pan of paint.

3. Give each child a paint smock, a sheet of blue construction paper, and a tree trunk. Help the children glue the tree trunks on their papers. Then show them how to dip their sponges into the paint and make leaves on their trees. Encourage them to take turns using different colors of paint.

4. As the paintings dry, give the children the Zaccheus figures and let them scribble color the figures. When the paint has dried on their trees, show the children how to take Zaccheus in and out of the tree.

WHAT YOU TALK ABOUT

Who was Jesus' friend in the story?
Who do you see in this room who is Jesus' friend?
Raise your hand if you are Jesus' friend.

Peanut Butter Play Dough

WHAT YOU NEED
Peanut butter
Powdered milk
Honey
Items to add to play dough, such as chopped nuts, raisins, M&Ms
Small Ziploc bags (two for each child)
Jesus stickers
Marker

WHAT YOU DO

1. Before craft time, make peanut butter play dough. For every four children, combine 2 cups peanut butter, 2 cups powdered milk, and 3 tablespoons honey. Add more powdered milk if the dough is still sticky.

2. Direct children to wash their hands. Give children lumps of play dough and allow them to choose what they will add to their dough (nuts, raisins, M&Ms, and so on).

3. Give children the Ziploc bags and ask them to use stickers to decorate their bags. Help them divide their dough into two sections and put it in the bags. On one bag, print their name. On the other bag, print the name of a friend with whom they will share the dough.

WHAT YOU TALK ABOUT
What meal did Jesus share with His friends?
With what friend can you share your dough?
Who is Jesus' friend?

Rhythm Bells

WHAT YOU NEED

Clothespins
Jingle bells (2 large bells for each child)
Marker
Glue
10" lengths of kite string

WHAT YOU DO

1. Dip the ends of the string in glue and allow the glue to dry. Print "Sing to Jesus" down the side of each clothespin.

2. Help children string the bells, then wrap the string tightly around the clothespin and knot securely. Apply a drop of glue to each knot to make it stronger.

WHAT YOU TALK ABOUT

Who sang to Jesus in the story?
Let's use our jingle bells and sing a song to Jesus!

Songbook

WHAT YOU NEED

Construction paper
Glue
Old music
Music note stickers
Markers
Crayons

WHAT TO DO

1 Fold sheets of construction paper in half. Print "My Jesus Songbook" on the front of each piece of folded paper.

2 Allow children to choose music to glue on the insides of their cards. They can use stickers and crayons to decorate the front of their cards.

3 Allow children to hold their songbooks and pretend to read the music as they sing favorite songs about Jesus.

WHAT YOU TALK ABOUT

What did the children in the story do to praise Jesus?
What songs can you sing to Jesus?

Rhythm Instrument

What you need

Small oatmeal or cornmeal boxes,
    one for each child
Hole punch
30" lengths of heavy string or cord
Glue or tape
Spring-type clothespins
Tempera paint and wide brushes
Painting smocks
Fun stickers (optional)

WHAT YOU DO

1 Punch holes about 1" down from the top of the boxes on opposite sides. String pieces of cord through both holes and tie the ends together inside the boxes. Glue or tape the lids on the boxes.

2 Let children paint the boxes. Allow time for the paint to dry. Children may put stickers on the boxes when the paint is dry.

3 Let children use the clothespins as drumsticks as you sing a thank-You song to Jesus. The drumsticks can be fastened to the cord for easy storage.

WHAT YOU TALK ABOUT

Who sang to Jesus?
What songs do you like to sing to Jesus?
Let's sing a thank-You song to Jesus.

Food Tray

WHAT YOU NEED
Styrofoam meat or vegetable trays
  one for each child
12" lengths of yarn
Tape
Pictures of food cut from
  magazines
Glue sticks
Crayons

WHAT YOU DO
1. Print on each tray "Thank You, God."

2. Let children choose foods they like to glue to their trays.

3. Help each child tape yarn to the back of the tray for a hanger.

WHAT YOU TALK ABOUT
What did Jesus thank God for in the story?
What foods will you thank God for?

Good-News Telephones

WHAT YOU NEED

Styrofoam cups, two for each child
3' lengths of yarn
Crayons
Stickers about Jesus

WHAT TO DO

1. Use a sharpened pencil or scissors to poke a hole in the bottom of each cup. Print on the cups, "Jesus Is Our Friend."

2. Guide children to decorate their cups with crayons and stickers. Help the children put their yarn through the holes in their cups and knot the ends inside the cups.

3. Show children how to talk into one end of their telephones while someone listens on the other end.

WHAT YOU TALK ABOUT

What good news did we learn about Jesus today? Use your telephone to tell a friend Jesus is alive! What other things could you tell about Jesus?

"Jesus is our Friend!"

Felt Jesus Pennant

WHAT YOU NEED
White or light-colored felt
Scraps of braid or trim
Paper
Crayons
Marker
Glue
Pennant pattern and Jesus card
 from page 148

WHAT YOU DO

1 Cut pennants out of felt. Photocopy and cut out the Jesus cards. Cut strips of braid or trim the right length to be glued to the left side of the pennant.

2 Guide children to color the Jesus cards and glue them on the pennant. Then help them glue the trim on the left side of the pennants.

WHAT YOU TALK ABOUT
Who listened to Jesus in the story?
Where do we read about what Jesus said?

WANT TO DO MORE?
Let children decorate their pennants with glitter glue.

Touch-and-Feel Picture

WHAT YOU NEED

Light brown and light blue
   construction paper
Copy paper
Fabric scraps
Orange, red, and yellow yarn
Small twigs
Glue
Sand
Jesus and disciples patterns from
   page 149

WHAT YOU DO

1 Cut strips of light blue paper and glue them across the tops of sheets of light brown construction paper. Copy and cut out the patterns of Jesus and the disciples from page 149. Cut twigs into small pieces and cut yarn into ½" to 1" pieces.

2 Help children glue the figures of Jesus and the disciples on their papers. Then show them how to glue fabric scraps on the figures for clothing. Place a puddle of glue on each paper where the fire should go. Then help the children add small twigs and yarn scraps to make the fire. Then put glue on the brown part of the pictures and let children sprinkle on sand. Gently shake off excess sand into a box lid to prevent spilling sand on the floor.

WHAT YOU TALK ABOUT

What did Jesus and His friends eat together?
Why were Jesus' friends happy?

Coin Pictures

WHAT YOU NEED
White paper
Lightweight aluminum foil
Various coins
Tape
Construction paper

WHAT YOU DO

1. Give children the white paper and help them tape it to the table. Then let them choose several coins that they want in their picture. Put rolled up tape on the backs of the coins and let them place them on the paper.

2. Give children pieces of aluminum foil. Help them lay the foil over the coins. Show them how to rub with their fingers or other blunt objects to make the coin shapes appear on their foil.

3. When the children have completed their pictures, help them carefully tape the foil to a piece of construction paper to help preserve it.

WHAT YOU TALK ABOUT
Who asked Peter and John for some money?
What did Peter give the lame man instead of money?

Finger Puppets

WHAT YOU NEED

Heavy paper
Scissors
Crayons
Barnabas and child finger puppets
   from page 137

WHAT YOU DO

1. Copy the puppets on heavy paper. Cut out a Barnabas and a child puppet for each child. Cut out the finger holes on the puppets.

2. Let children color their puppets. Then show them how to put their fingers through the holes to make legs for the puppets. Let them practice making their puppets walk and jump and run.

WHAT YOU TALK ABOUT

How did Barnabas help? Use your Barnabas puppet to pretend to help.
What nice things can you say to your friends?
Use your puppet to act out what you will say to your friend.

Flannel Face

WHAT YOU NEED
Two colors of flannel or felt
Envelopes
Glue
Red yarn
Head and features patterns from
   page 136

WHAT YOU DO

1. Enlarge the pattern. Cut heads from one color of flannel or felt. Make sure you cut both boy and girl heads (girls have the longer hair). Cut facial features from another color of flannel or felt. Print "_____ learns from the Bible" at one end of each envelope.

2. Print each child's name in the blank as you give the children the envelopes. Help the children glue the heads on the envelopes. Then let children arrange the facial features on the face. Show the children how to store the facial features in their envelopes.

WHAT YOU TALK ABOUT
What can you use to see and read the Bible?
What can you use to listen to the Bible?
What can you use to ask questions about the Bible?

learns from
the Bible

Framed Silhouettes

WHAT YOU NEED

Black, white, and colored construction paper
Glue
Tape
Bright lamp, flashlight, or overhead projector
Pencil
Stickers
Pieces of colored construction paper, foil, cloth, trim
Glue

WHAT YOU DO

1. Cut oval frames from various colors of construction paper. Make the frames no more than 1" wide at the sides and ends. Print at the bottom, "Jesus' Helper."

2. Seat a child close to a blank wall. Shine a bright light on the wall. Tape a sheet of black construction paper where the child's shadow falls. Move the light around until you get a clear silhouette. Trace around this with pencil on the black construction paper. Cut out the silhouette.

3. As you work on the silhouettes, allow children to decorate their frames with stickers and pieces of paper, foil, or cloth.

4. Help children glue the silhouettes on the white paper. Then help them center the silhouettes in the frames and glue them.

WHAT YOU TALK ABOUT

Who did Paul talk to when he saw a bright light?
How did Paul help Jesus?
Who can you tell about Jesus?

102

Dusting Mitt

WHAT YOU NEED

Flannel or other soft cloth
Needle and thread or sewing
    machine
Felt
Glue
Scissors
Yarn
Mitt and features patterns from
    page 137

WHAT YOU DO

1. Enlarge the patterns. Cut two pieces of the mitt pattern from flannel for each child. Cut two eyes from felt and a 2" piece of yarn for the mouth for each child.

2. Sew the mitts together, leaving the wrist edge open. If you cannot stitch them, use white glue around the edges. Give them adequate time to dry completely.

3. Show children how to glue the eyes and mouth onto their mitts. Let them practice dusting with their mitt. The mitt will work best if the children wear the face side on the backs of their hands.

WHAT YOU TALK ABOUT

Who helped in our story?
What can you do with your mitt to help?

refrigerator magnets

WHAT YOU NEED

Poster board
Strip magnets
Spring-type clothespins
Index cards
Glue
Praying hands pattern from page
    136

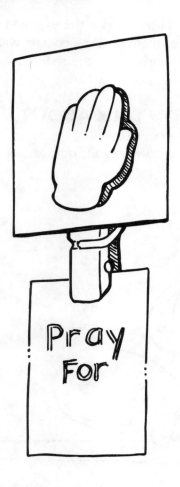

Pray For

WHAT YOU DO

1 Trace the praying hands onto poster board, one for each child. Print "pray for" on index cards, one for each child.

2 Help children glue the praying hands on clothespins. Show them how to put the praying hands face down on the table, apply glue to the top half of the clothespins, and then place it on the hands and hold in place for a few minutes.

3 Help children remove the paper backing from small pieces of strip magnets and attach them to the back of the clothespin.

4 Give children the index cards and show them how to clip them onto the magnet. Demonstrate how the magnet will stick to a metal surface, such as the refrigerator.

WHAT YOU TALK ABOUT

Who did the Christians pray for in our story?
Who do you pray for?
Ask your Mom and Dad to put the magnet on the refrigerator to remind your family to pray.

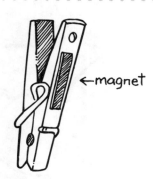

←magnet

Helping Hearts

WHAT YOU NEED

Various colors of poster board
White paper
Bits of ribbon, lace, old buttons, and
    other decorative items to glue
    on the hearts
Tacky glue
Scissors
Hole punch
Ribbon
Heart and frame pattern from page
    149

WHAT YOU DO

1. Cut two heart frames out of poster board for each child. Also cut hearts from white paper. Print "Thank you for teaching me to be Jesus' helper" on the hearts.

2. Help children glue a white heart between two poster board frames. Then allow them to decorate the fronts of their heart frames with the items you provide.

3. Punch a hole in the top of each heart and tie a ribbon through the hole for a hanger.

WHAT YOU TALK ABOUT

Who taught Timothy to be Jesus' helper?
Who teaches you to be Jesus' helper?
Give them your heart to say thank-you.

Cut and remove inside for frame

Thank you for teaching me to be Jesus' helper.

Jesus Sewing Card

WHAT YOU NEED

Lightweight cardboard or poster
 board
36" lengths of yarn
Glue
Marker
Purple crayons
Hole punch
Tape
Pictures of Jesus from old materials
 or copies of the picture of Jesus
 from page 148

WHAT YOU DO

1 Cut 6½" squares from the cardboard. Punch holes around the edges, not more than 4-5 holes to a side. Dip the ends of the yarn in glue, twist, and let dry. Print on the squares "Jesus loves you."

2 Let children color their squares with the purple crayons. Help them glue on their pictures of Jesus.

3 Show children how to "sew" around the edges of their cards. Tape the yarn that is left to the back of the card to make a hanger.

WHAT YOU TALK ABOUT

Who sold purple cloth for sewing in our Bible story?
Who did Paul tell Lydia about?
Who can you tell about Jesus?

Cardboard Telephone

WHAT YOU NEED
5" x 7" pieces of poster board
Toilet tissue rolls
String or cord
Marker
Hole punch

WHAT YOU DO

1 Draw a circle on each piece of poster board and print the words "I can talk to God!" as shown in the illustration. Punch a hole in the side of the poster board and in the end of the tube.

2 Guide children to color the poster board and the tubes. Then help them attach a string through both holes. Show the children how to hold the tube to their ear as they pretend to talk into the circle on the board.

WHAT YOU TALK ABOUT
Who talked to God in the Bible story?
What do you say when you talk to God?
Let's pretend to use our telephones as we talk to God.

switch-plate Picture

WHAT YOU NEED

Two colors of self-adhesive plastic
Permanent marker
Switch plate and flower patterns
   from page 136

WHAT YOU DO

1. Cut the switch-plate covers from one color of plastic. Cut three flowers for each child from another color of plastic. Print the words "Read the Bible" on the flowers, one word on each flower.

2. Give children the flowers, one at a time, in the order in which the words appear. Help them stick the words in order to their switch plates.

3. Tell children to have their parents help them stick the cover on their light switch at home. You may wish to send a note home, explaining the project to the parents.

WHAT YOU TALK ABOUT

Who read the Bible in our story today?
Who can you ask to read the Bible to you?

Jesus' Helper Necklace

WHAT YOU NEED

Potato chip can lids or other small
    plastic lids
Construction paper
24" lengths of yarn
O-shaped cereal
Hole punch
Glue
Small safety pins
Pictures of Jesus from old materials
    or copies of the Jesus picture
    from page 148

WHAT YOU DO

1. Cut 2" construction paper circles. On each circle, print "Jesus' Helper." Dip the ends of the yarn into glue, twist, and let dry.

2. Give each child a plastic lid, construction-paper circle, length of yarn, and picture of Jesus. Show children how to glue the construction-paper circle inside their lids. Then they should glue the picture of Jesus onto the construction paper.

3. Punch holes at the tops of the lids. Let the children string 10-12 pieces of cereal onto the yarn. Then use a safety pin to attach the lid to the yarn. Then have children string 10-12 more pieces of cereal onto the yarn. Help each child tie the yarn into a knot.

WHAT YOU TALK ABOUT

How did the people on the island help Paul?
What did Paul do for a sick man on the island?
How can you be Jesus' helper?

milk-Carton watering Can

WHAT YOU NEED

plastic milk carton with handles
  (one for each child)
ice pick
colored self-adhesive plastic
eyes and mouth patterns from
  page 133

WHAT YOU DO

1 Cut out eyes and smile patterns from self-adhesive plastic. With an ice pick, poke holes in the corner of each plastic jug, opposite the handle. See the illustration.

2 Show the children how to make a happy face on their watering cans by sticking on the self-adhesive mouth below the holes in the plastic jug and the eyes on either side of the holes.

WHAT YOU TALK ABOUT

Who helped in our Bible story?
How can you help?

Bible Megaphone

WHAT YOU NEED

Heavy construction paper or
    poster board
Waxed milk cartons
Tempera paint
Large bristle brush
Painting smocks
X-acto knife
Tape
Megaphone and Bible word pattern
    from page 135

WHAT YOU DO

1. Use the pattern on page 135 to cut megaphones out of heavy paper or poster board. Draw a straight line on each megaphone and print the words "learns from the" under it. See the illustration. Make stencils of the word Bible using the pattern. Cut the stencils from a waxed milk carton with an X-acto knife. Make one stencil for every 2-3 children.

2. Print each child's name on the line on the megaphone. Allow children to use the stencils to paint the word "Bible" under your printed words. Have children wear painting smocks to protect their clothing. Tape the stencil in place on the megaphone. Then let children paint.

3. When the paint is dry, help children tape their megaphones into shape.

WHAT YOU TALK ABOUT

Who heard about the Bible in our story?
What are some Bible stories you have heard?
Tell about the stories using your megaphone.

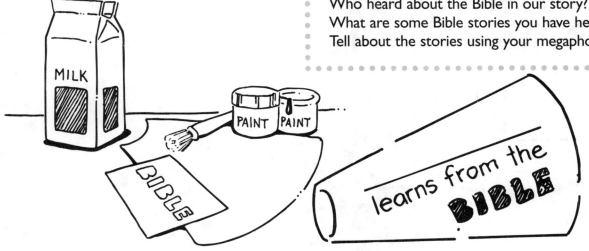

Church Building Puzzle

WHAT YOU NEED

Dinner-size paper plates
Glue
Marker
Crayons
Scissors
Church building pattern from page
   133 or pictures of your church

WHAT YOU DO

1. Print "Come to church" on the outer edges of the plates. Copy and cut out a church for each child.

2. Let children color the plates and church pictures. Then help them glue the pictures on the plates.

3. Make puzzles by cutting the plates into 3 or 4 pieces. Print each child's name on the puzzle pieces. Allow time for the children to play with their puzzles.

WHAT YOU TALK ABOUT

Who was Jesus' helper in our story?
How can you be Jesus' helper?
Who can you invite to church?

Sugar Dough Hearts

WHAT YOU NEED

Sugar dough (1 cup water, 2 cups sugar, 3 cups flour)
Red food coloring
Peppermint extract
Glitter
Various heart cookie cutters
Pink, white or red ribbon
Scissors

WHAT YOU DO

1. Knead the sugar, flour, and water together. Then add red food coloring to make red or pink dough. Add a few drops of peppermint extract to make it smell nice. If you wish, add glitter to the dough to make it sparkly.

2. Give each child a lump of dough. Show them how to pat the dough out to flatten it. Then help them cut a heart shape out of the dough, using a cookie cutter.

3. Use the point of the scissors to make a small hole in the top of each heart. Then bake the hearts in a 275-300° oven until hard.

4. When the hearts have cooled, help children string pieces of ribbon through the holes and tie them.

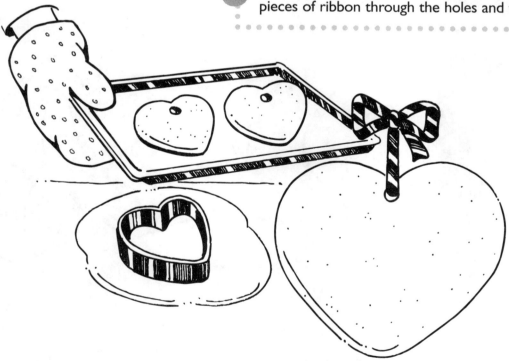

Bunny place card

WHAT YOU NEED
Pastel poster board
Scissors
Curly ribbon
Paper hole punch
Marshmallow bunnies
Marker

WHAT YOU DO

1. Cut egg shapes from 2½" x 4" pieces of poster board.

2. Give each child an egg shape and print his name at the top of the card.

3. Punch two holes, help children thread curly ribbon through the holes, and tie a marshmallow bunny to the card. The ribbon should be around the bunny's neck.

4. Curl the ribbon. Trim the bottom of the egg card to make the bunny stand.

Jason — cut bottom

Mary

Eggshell garden

WHAT YOU NEED
Styrofoam egg cartons
Scissors
Cotton balls
Grass seed
Markers
Easter stickers
Sandwich bags

WHAT YOU DO

1. Cut the tops off the egg cartons, and cut the bottoms into six sections.

2. Give children the egg carton sections and guide them to decorate the outside with markers and stickers.

3. Help children put a moistened cotton ball in each empty egg slot and sprinkle grass seed on the cotton.

4. Allow children to put their gardens into a sandwich bag for safe travel home. You may wish to send a short note home, explaining that the cotton must be kept moist for the seeds to grow.

Flower necklace

WHAT YOU NEED

36" pieces of yarn
Foam egg cups cut from egg
    cartons (12 for each necklace)
Plastic straws
Poster board
Scissors
Flower stickers or other pretty
    stickers
Perfume (optional)
Glue
Hole punch

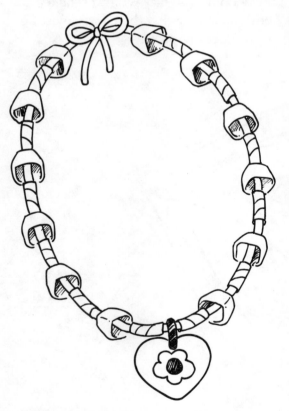

WHAT YOU DO

1 Dip the ends of the yarn in glue and let dry to make it easier to string. Cut straws into $1\frac{7}{8}$" pieces. With scissors, make a hole in the bottom center of each egg cup.

2 Cut circles or hearts out of poster board for pendants for the necklace. Punch a hole in the top of each shape.

3 Assemble the parts for a necklace for each child: 12 egg cups, a piece of yarn, 13 straw pieces, and a pendant.

4 Guide children to decorate their pendants with stickers. If you wish, place a drop of perfume on the pendants.

5 Help children string the pendants on their yarn first. Then help them alternate stringing straws and egg cups on both sides of the pendants. Don't worry if they don't string exactly in order or evenly.

6 Help children tie the ends of Mom's necklace together.

stationery

WHAT YOU NEED

White or pastel paper
Construction paper
Pinking shears
Watercolors
Large paintbrushes
Cups
Smocks
Newspaper
Crayons

WHAT YOU DO

1. Cut sheets of 8½ x 11" paper in half and cut around the edges with pinking shears. Make four or five sheets of paper for each child. Fold sheets of construction paper in half. Print "For Mom" on the front of each folded piece.

2. Cover the work area with newspaper. Fill cups with water and set out paints and brushes. Help children put on paint smocks.

3. Guide children to paint their sheets of paper. They do not need to draw pictures with the paints. They can simply cover the papers with wide strokes of paint. They may use one color or several different colors.

4. Give each child a folded piece of construction paper and print their names on the front. Allow them to color the construction paper folder as their paintings dry.

5. Help children put the stationery in the folders to take home to Mom.

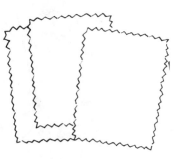

Tie Bookmark

WHAT YOU NEED

Cardboard or poster board
Scissors
Glue
9" pieces of yarn
Tie pattern from page 154

WHAT YOU DO

1 Cut four tie patterns from cardboard or poster board for each child. Print on the ties as shown in the illustration.

2 Help children glue two ties together on each end of the piece of yarn, sandwiching the yarn between the ties.

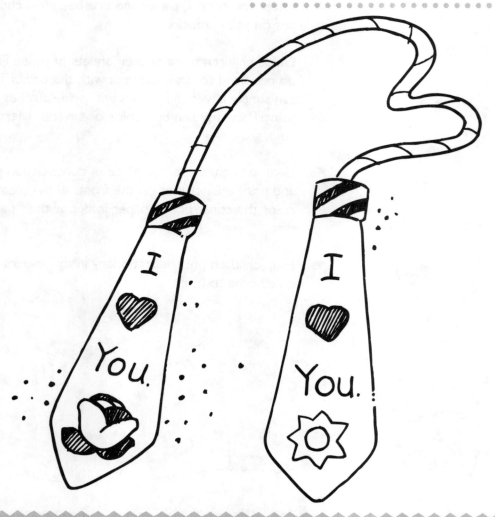

Magnetic Picture Frame

WHAT YOU NEED
Poster board
Crayons
Stickers
Scissors
Self-sticking magnetic strips
Instant camera or photo of each
     child
Glue

WHAT TO DO

1. Cut two poster board picture frames for each child. Cut four magnetic strips for each child.

2. Take instant pictures of the children to use in the frames or collect pictures ahead of time.

3. Guide children to decorate one poster board frame, using crayons and stickers. Then help children glue the frames together with the picture between.

4. Help children stick four magnetic strips to the back of their frames.

stars & stripes picture

WHAT YOU NEED

White paper
Dark blue crayons
Red tempera paint
Large paintbrushes
Old newspapers
Paint smocks
Star pattern from page 154

WHAT TO DO

1 Trace several star outlines onto white pieces of paper for each child.

2 Cover tables with newspaper and help children into paint smocks. Place tempera paint in aluminum pie pans in the center of the table.

3 First help children color around the stars with blue crayon. Then show them how to make red stripes on their paper across the stars, using the red tempera paint.

Pilgrim Hats

WHAT YOU NEED

White and black construction
    paper (12" x 18")
Stapler
Scissors
Buckle pattern from page 154

WHAT YOU DO

1 Cut girl hat patterns from white paper and boy hat patterns from black paper. Use the sketches below to guide you as you cut the hats. Cut buckles from white paper, using the pattern.

2 Help children fold and staple their hats.

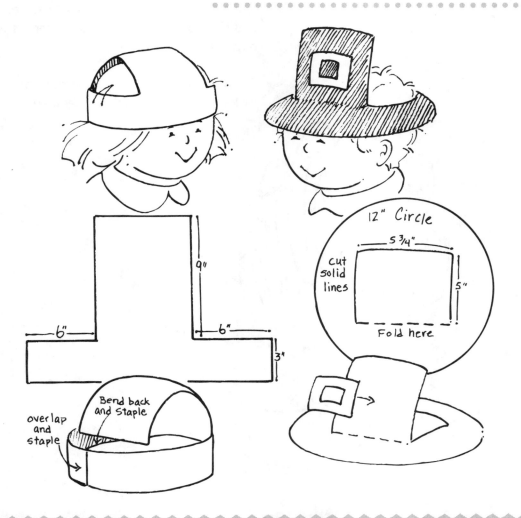

9"

6"   6"

3"

overlap
and
staple

Bend back
and staple

12" Circle

5 ¾"

cut
solid
lines

5"

Fold here

Glove Turkey Puppets

WHAT YOU NEED

Small mittens, one for each child
Fabric glue
Crayons
Scissors
Turkey head and feather patterns
    from page 154

WHAT YOU DO

1. Copy and cut out a turkey head and feathers for each child.

2. Allow children to color their turkey heads and feathers in bright colors.

3. Help children lay their mittens down, palm side up. Guide them to glue the turkey heads to the thumbs and the feathers to where their fingers will go in the mittens. Allow the glue to dry.

4. Show children how to put on their mittens and make their turkeys walk and gobble.

wreath

WHAT YOU NEED

6" paper plates
Stiff paste, made with powdered
    sugar and a little water
Cotton swabs
Spearmint candy leaves
Red gumdrops
Christmas stickers
Glue
Marker

WHAT YOU DO

1 Help children paste eight spearmint leaves on the plates to form a wreath. Paste two red gumdrops at the top. Allow paste to dry.

2 Allow children to decorate their wreaths with Christmas stickers and help them print their names at the tops of the wreaths.

star votives

WHAT YOU NEED
Tea lights candles
Clear, votive candle holders
Small star stickers

WHAT YOU DO

1. Guide children to decorate their votive holders with star stickers.

2. Help each child place a tea light in his holder.

3. Show children the star shadows when the candle is lit.

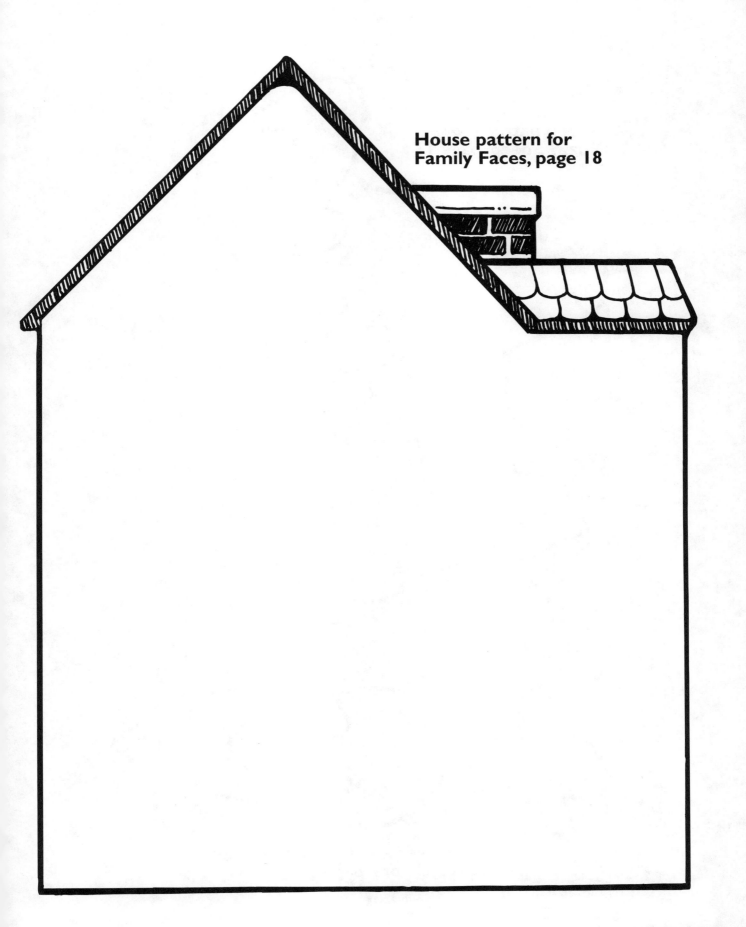

**House pattern for
Family Faces, page 18**

125

**Sheep pattern for
Fuzzy Sheep, page 13**

**Star, flower, and bird patterns for
Glitter Colors, page 12**

Jesus card for Our Best Friend Hearts, page 21

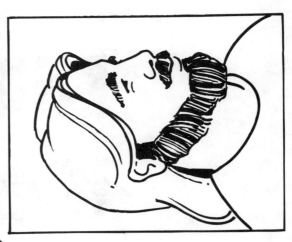

Squirrel pattern for Squirrels, page 28

Naaman pattern for Naaman puppet, page 43

Police

Fireman

Fire and police badge patterns for Helping Hats, page 26

Clock hands pattern for Clocks, page 28

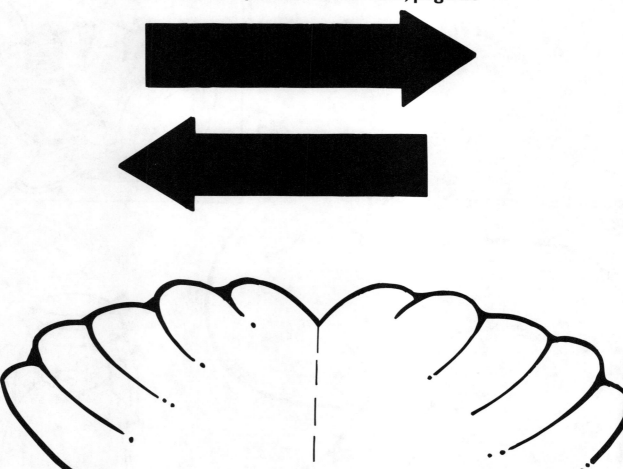

Bird and wings pattern for Flying Birds, page 23

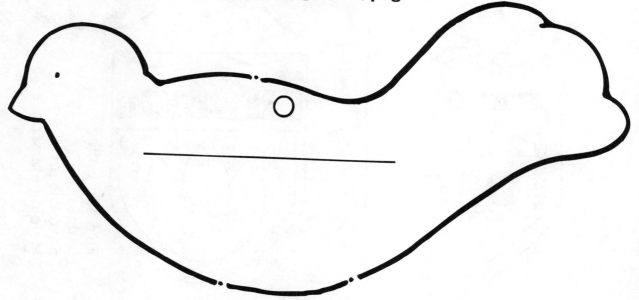

128

Dear_____,
    I learned some good news today.
    Jesus was born!
    I would like you to come to church with me, so you can hear the good news about Jesus too.
                    Love,

Letter and pictures for Good-News Letters, page 54

Boy pattern for Boy Puppet, page 69

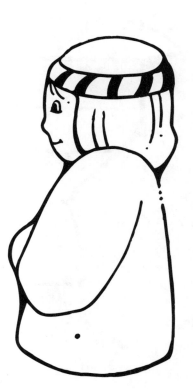

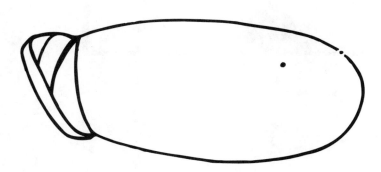

129

**Manger and baby patterns for
Baby Jesus Picture, page 57**

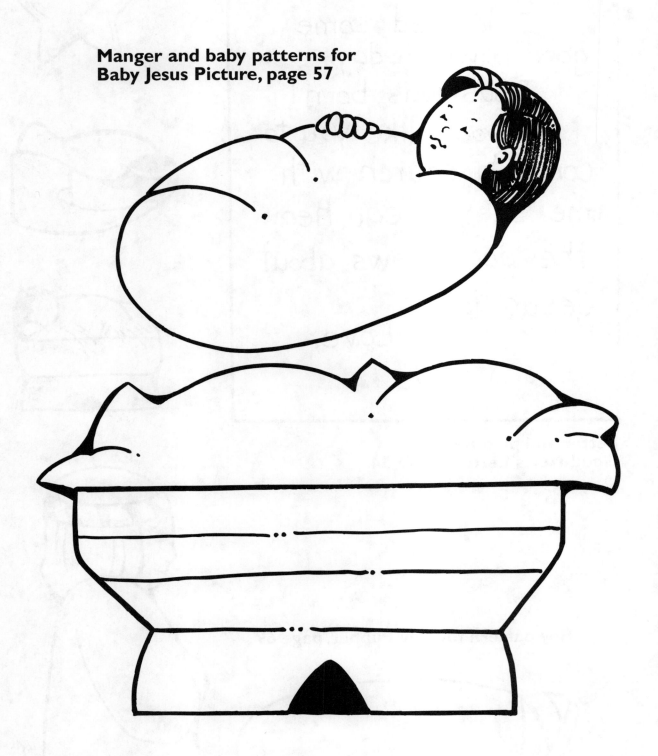

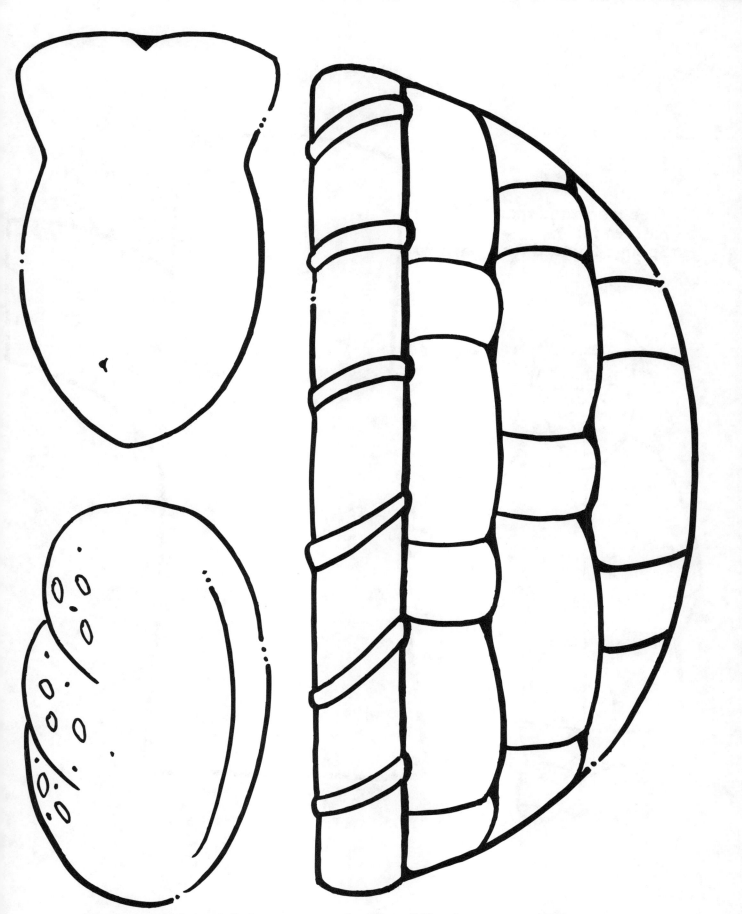

Basket, loaf, and fish patterns for Food Baskets, page 79

131

**Tree trunk and man
pattern for
Sponge-Painted Tree, page 90**

Puppet for Stick Puppets, page 66

**Eyes and mouth for
Milk-Carton Watering Can, page 110**

**Church building for
Church Building Puzzle, page 112**

133

LOVE EACH OTHER ♡.

John 15:17

WE PRAY TO GOD

2 Corinthians 13:7

LOVE GOD ♡.

Mark 12:30

Bible words cards for Envelope Bible, page 70

134

BIBLE

**Megaphone and Bible word pattern for
Bible Megaphone, page 111**

135

READ

THE

BIBLE

Switch plate and flower patterns for
Switch-plate Picture, page 108

**Head and features patterns for
Flannel Face, page 101**

**Praying hands pattern for
Refrigerator Magnet, page 104**

Barnabas and child finger puppets for page 100

Glue or Stitch Edges

Mitt and features patterns for Dusting Mitt, page 103

Star pattern for Star Chain Decoration, page 56

**Sheep, baby, star, and angel patterns for
Christmas Surprise Rubbings, page 60**

138

Hearts for Heart Hanging, page 76

139

Flower patterns for Thank-You Card, page 33

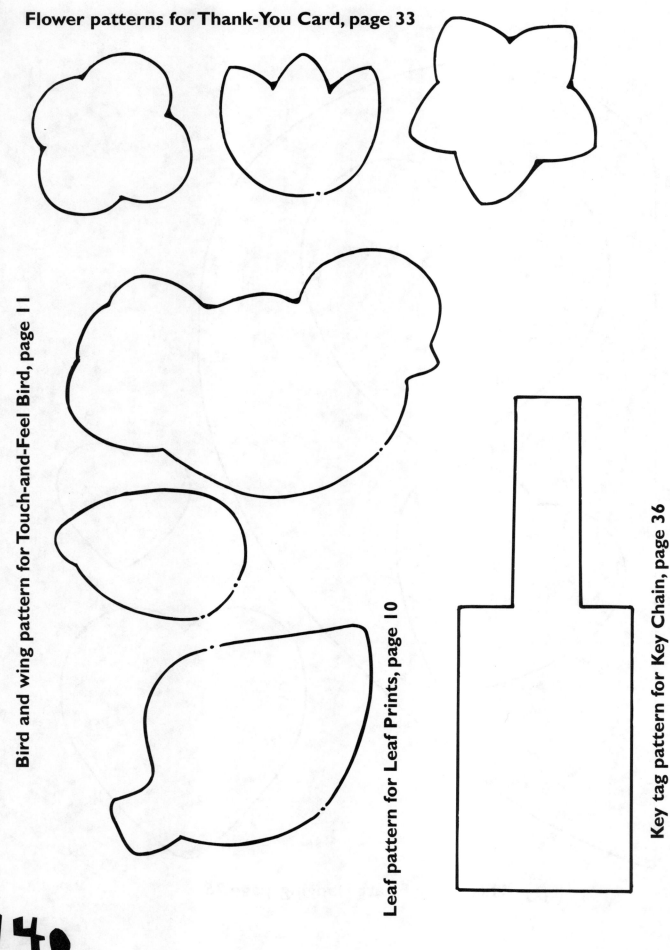

Bird and wing pattern for Touch-and-Feel Bird, page 11

Leaf pattern for Leaf Prints, page 10

Key tag pattern for Key Chain, page 36

140

Dolls and clothing for Paper Dolls, page 17

141

God Gives Us Houses

Corn husk pattern for Corn on the Cob, page 40

T-shirt pattern for Personalized T-shirt, page 34

**Arrow for
Prayer Spinner, page 39**

Arrow and pictures for Obey Chart, page 65

Boat and sail patterns for Bathtub Boats, page 78

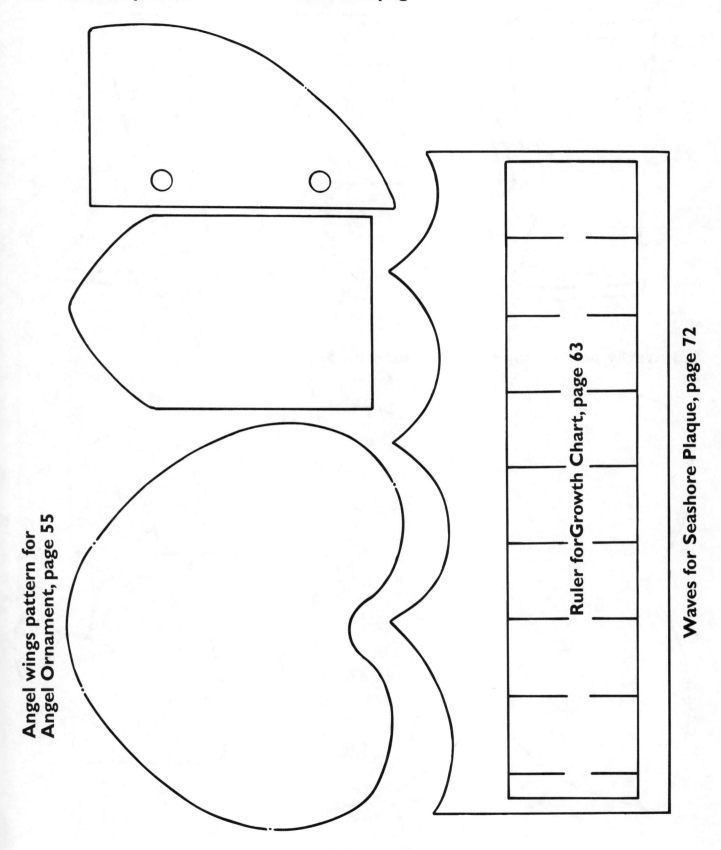

Angel wings pattern for
Angel Ornament, page 55

Ruler forGrowth Chart, page 63

Waves for Seashore Plaque, page 72

145

Child and legs pattern for Legs Picture, page 74

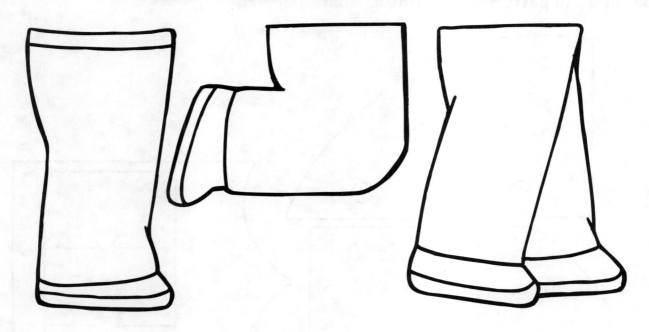

Butterfly pattern for Floating Butterfly, page 89

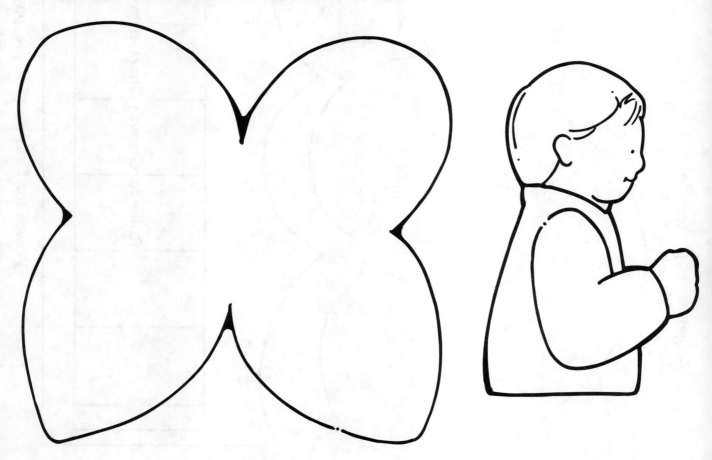

146

Face pattern for Sad or Glad Face, page 75

147

Pennant and Jesus card for Felt Jesus Pennant, page 97

We Listen to Him.

Jesus and children patterns for "Come to Me" Picture, page 86

148

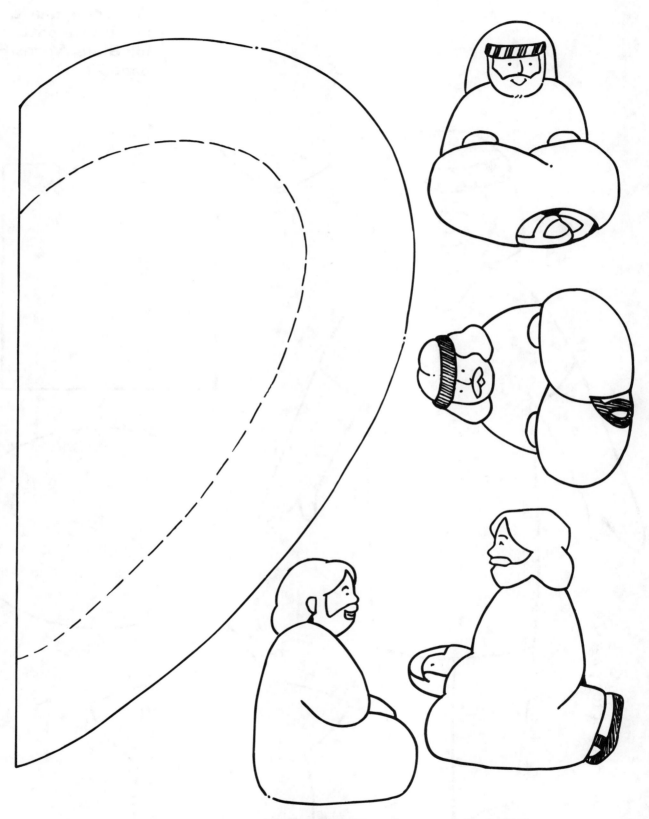

Heart and frame pattern for Helping Hearts, page 105

**Jesus and disciples patterns for
Touch-and-Feel Picture, page 98**

149

Oval, star, heart, and house patterns for Bible Words Puzzle, page 22

Joseph Puppet for page 24

**Worship pictures for
Worship Foldout, page 31**

**Doll pattern for
Paper Doll Friends, page 32**

I am
a Church
Helper

**Pendant pattern for Church
Helper Necklace, page 35**

1⁵2

**Heart pattern for
Our Best Friend Hearts, page 21**

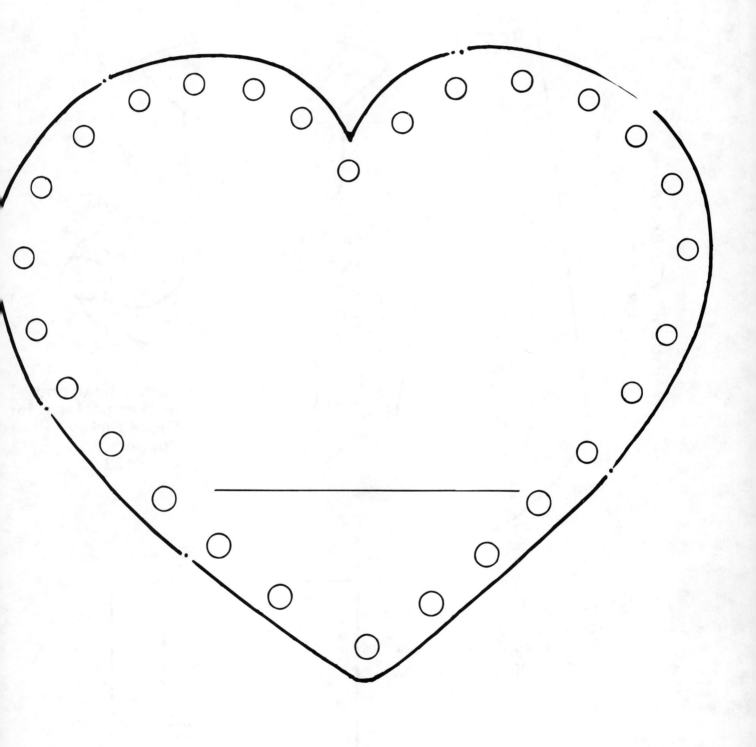

153

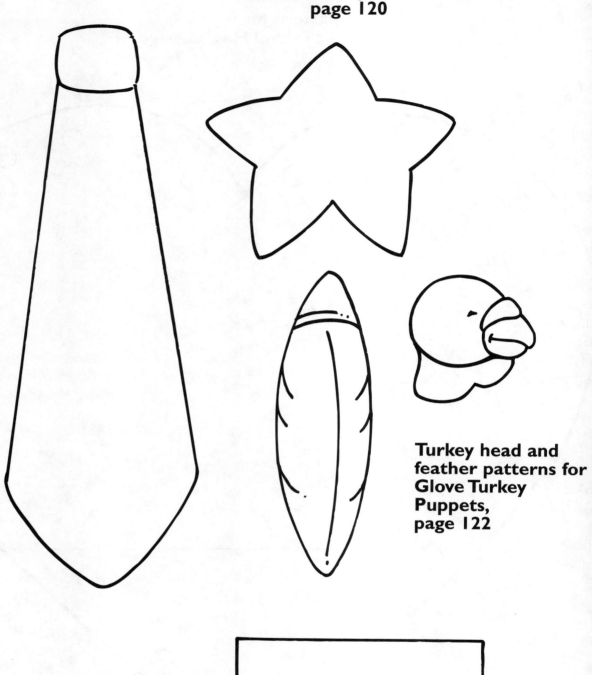

Tie pattern for Tie Bookmark,
page 118

Turkey head and
feather patterns for
Glove Turkey
Puppets,
page 122

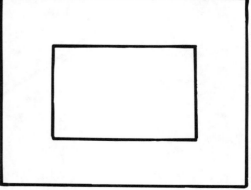

Buckle pattern for
Pilgrim Hats
page 121

154

Index

Index

2's & 3's Curriculum Syllabus

The following pages list stories from Standard Publishing's 2's and 3's Sunday School curriculum, along with the crafts that match each story.

2's & 3's Curriculum Syllabus

2's & 3's Curriculum Syllabus